HOPE
for the Mainline Church

HOPE for the Mainline Church

Charles Bayer

CBP Press
St. Louis, Missouri

© Copyright 1991 CBP Press

All rights reserved. No part of this book may be reproduced without written permission from CBP Press, Box 179, St. Louis, MO 63166.

Quotations marked NRSV are from the New Revised Standard Version Bible, copyrighted 1989, Division of Christian Education of the National Council of Churches in the United States of America and are used by permission.

Library of Congress Cataloging-in-Publication

Bayer, Charles H.
    Hope for the mainline church.
        1. Liberalism (Religion)—United States—Protestant churches. 2. Church growth—United States. 3. Interdenominational cooperation—United States. 4. Church Renewal. 5. Middle classes—United States—Religious life. I. Title. II. Title: Hope for the mainline church.
BR526.B39   1991   280'.4'0973   90-20411
ISBN 0-8272-1424-3

*Dedicated to Wendy
who rarely lets me get away with fluffy answers
or uneasy compromises*

Contents

1. Can the Mainline Church Survive? — 1
2. Care and Courage — 9
3. The Pastoral and the Prophetic — 19
4. Jerusalem and the Ends of the Earth — 29
5. Being In and Of the World — 41
6. Church Growth and a Radical Faith — 49
7. Two Flags—Two Loyalties — 59
8. A Sending and a Receiving Church — 65
9. A Recovery of the Sacred — 75
10. Lessons from Liberation — 89
11. New Issues for a New Age — 103
12. Come Life or Death — 111

1

Can the Mainline Church Survive?

Mainline denominations are in serious trouble. They are losing numerical strength and persuasive power year after year. The most optimistic word one hears is, "We think things have bottomed out," or "The rate of decline seems to have slowed." Nevertheless, things continue to deteriorate, and the bottom may not yet be in sight. A casual look through the yearbooks of most of the ecumenically minded denominations confirms that the United Methodist, Presbyterian, United Church of Christ, Christian Church (Disciples of Christ), American Baptist, Episcopal and other like-minded denominations have taken a series of body blows from which some predict they may not recover.

These denominations had long been the backbone of America's liberal religious tradition. Their leading pastors were widely known and respected. Their parishes were welcomed in every city and town. The colleges and seminaries they planted, first for the education of the clergy and then for wider intellectual pursuits, provided the academic foundations of the culture.

Until a few years ago the appeal of mainline bodies was general and their growth steady. Sometime in the late 60s, however, the tide turned. A new religious style emerged, whose highly visible advocates began to seize the attention of the American people. The advocates had learned from old-time radio evangelists how to use mass media, and from modern marketers how to use computerized mailings. They often appealed to the popular fears and prejudices of people who saw themselves on a dangerous international sea, with an ominous red storm boiling ever closer to the coast of the homeland. They claimed that if Christian America was the citadel of democracy, meaning anti-communism, the preservation of "our way of life" was a religious imperative. They had simple—often one-verse—answers to everything. There were no gray areas. The substance of faith was clear and unambiguous.

The mainline denominations stood on the sideline and observed this phenomenon with increasing dismay. Not only had the new breed stolen the spotlight, but the mainliners became aware that they were unable to halt the erosion of their own vitality.

At almost every denominational gathering, the loss of strength is now the main topic of conversation. Convention speakers first lament the malaise and then call for a renewed commitment, which they believe can reverse the trend. Sprinkled in are exhortations to remember the heritage that made the body great, and fervent reminders that "we are a mighty people and have reason to hold our heads high."

Others insist we should stop talking about our problems on pragmatic grounds. They point out that negative talk never wins anybody. "Who in their right mind will board a sinking ship?"

And then there are private conversations where delegates talk quietly about our need to be more like church bodies crowded with the "born again." "All this liberalism, social action and church union talk is killing us!" So echo the hotel hallways, convention center corridors, and neighborhood coffee shops. "Why, that tabernacle across town draws two thousand people every Sunday. They believe the Bible and aren't afraid to say so."

Finally come our own new "evangelists," who insist that if we only learn to qualify our prospects and market properly, there is no reason we can't soon be stronger than we ever were.

Despite these stirring oratorical flights, brow-furrowed conversations, and suggested new strategies, at the next meeting of the assembly the data is even more dismal.

The issue is sharpened when we examine the congregations that make up these denominations. Parishes of immense strength a few years ago are either shadows of their former selves or have gone out of existence. Parishes carefully placed in prime locations, whose predicted growth was enormous, sit saddled with large building debts but without the numerical strength to handle the payments. Old First Church squats amid a decaying downtown in a monstrous, inefficient structure with the ancient ivy crawling slowly around the outside and the ancient congregation—or what is left of it—crawling slowly around the inside.

Parish leaders are just as confused as denominational officials. Unable to compete with the new breed of fundamentalists, the temptation has been either to mimic them, and turn sanctuaries into sound stages under a theological perspective that would make any thoughtful Christian wince, or to accept the trivialization of the marketers. In either case the inauthenticity of the enterprise eventually surfaces, and the ensuing pain is even more deeply felt. Hundreds of these congregations have gone out not with a shout but with a whimper.

Among "liberal" clergy, both old and young, there is a grimness which often approaches despair. They have a vision of the gospel, but the winds are wrong and the tides are wrong, and they sit on the shore and watch the vital waters of life slowly ebb until the beach is dry and sterile. A recent letter from one such minister illustrates the depth of the epidemic. He writes:

> Two years ago I became pastor of a new congregation in our city. But we haven't grown and we have serious financial problems. Our energy level is low and the newness has worn off. I don't know whether we can survive or not. Any advice?

This book is my response to that and to many other letters, calls, and conversations. The pages were born out of attending too many meetings of ministerial colleagues where I heard too many horror stories about decay, mistreatment, losing battles, loss of direction, and increased despair.

Obviously, much of the problem has to do with sociological factors only remotely connected to theological issues. The expected robustness of congregations newly planted a generation ago was predicated on statistics generated by the baby boomers. One reason Sunday school attendance has fallen off is that there are not as many children around these days. School districts in middle-class communities are experiencing similar declines in enrollment. It appears that the kind of people who tend to make up the typical mainline congregation are not as prolific as those in other sectors of the population. Twenty years ago it was "in" to talk about zero population growth. Well, we achieved it, and then asked, with open mouths and wide eyes, about the sparse attendance in our children's classes and youth groups.

Other cultural factors also play a significant role in the grayness of mainline church life. We are in the midst of a reaction to the sterility of religion that never moves from the mind to the body. If we often tend to be a dull cerebral lot, we are surrounded by religious expressions not captive of the life of the mind. Prejudice may have replaced reflection, and superstition may have eaten away at the vital organs of authentic faith. But it is exciting!

People want to be entertained, and let's face it, we are not very entertaining. Our worship is not "with it." We are disturbed if anything happens that is not carefully planned and faithfully printed. God can't do anything on Sunday morning that the church secretary doesn't have in writing by Thursday noon. Unlike the New Kids on the Block, there is not much applause at our performances, be they sermons or musical offerings. Nor do we stir the darker emotions by appealing to basic prejudices and fears. We are optimistic in outlook, that part of our older liberal tradition not being fully dismissed. And who can look hard at the world and not smile politely at the cockeyed optimists?

Middle-class society is far more secular than it was a generation ago. As a Methodist friend of mine commented, "The white you see when you cross the Rocky Mountains going west is not snow, but church letters tossed out of car windows at the continental divide." Whether we like to admit it or not, the official religion of this land is now secularism. We hear about godless communism, but there also exists an epidemic of godless capitalism, and the United States, following the lead of Europe, is the world headquarters.

If mainline denominations and their congregations are in trouble, so are the inter-church institutions they spawned. To keep the National Council of Churches or the World Council of Churches in our budgets takes repeated defensive effort. When things get tight, these line items are among the first to go. Budgets of most ecumenical bodies are in shambles. They have been forced to lay off staff, reduce programs, and spend time defending themselves. There are those who believe the National Council of Churches will be a historic curiosity by the turn of the century. Who has not heard the lament, "The only way we can balance the budget is to cut missions"?—and first to feel the knife are the ecumenical organizations.

One could carry on this distressful litany to book length. The question before us is, however: Shall we throw in the towel, give it over to the advertising strategies of the church growth movement, or see if we can mimic our more successful brothers and sisters without forfeiting our souls? Or is there another way?

I am convinced there is another way. We can be faithful, authentic, liberal, biblical, and be heard, effective, and dynamic. Not only is there hope for the mainline church, but our best days may be yet to come.

The root problem, and thus the radical solution, I believe to be theological, not sociological. Liberation theologians tell us that theology must be contextual. If it is impossible to transport, intact, what is thought about God from one culture to another, neither can theology be delivered whole from one era to another. "What is Christ for us today?" asked Dietrich Bonhoeffer. It is the refusal of mainline churches to pursue that question that lies at the core of our disease.

Local pastors, backed up by an informed and committed laity, are the church's front-line theologians. Reduced to being tour guides, masters of ceremony, chief operating officers, social directors, and protectors of the status quo, they can no longer articulate the meaning of the faith in word or action. Having lost its bearings, the mainline church defines itself more and more narrowly—taking care of its kind of people, doing a little social action, trying to run a solvent institution. In the process we have grown cautious. If there is a hole in the bottom of the grain bag, one tends to walk gingerly in an effort to see that the hole doesn't get any larger and the loss exacerbated.

Captives of our own carefulness, things get worse. A young pastor writes:

> I can't afford any more losses. If I wander beyond where my people are comfortable, there goes one more family. I'm down to rock bottom. The only thing I can do is sit quietly in the center of the boat and try not to make any waves. And I am miserable!

This sort of conservatism is the mark of a people who believe all their best days are behind them and who must therefore sit passively in rocking chairs, lest in moving about they fall, fracture a hip, and end up in a nursing home. That perspective is a commitment to death! Vital faith calls us to life! The Christian hope lies at the edges of life, at the borders of faith and action.

Creativity happens on the boundary. So said Paul Tillich in an autobiographical sketch published in 1966. In this intimate introspective analysis, Tillich described the dynamic edges on which his creativity was sharpened. "The boundary is the best place for acquiring knowledge," he had written earlier. Looking back over his life he concluded: "At almost every point, I have had to stand between alternative possibilities of existence, to be completely at home in neither and to take no definite stand against either....This disposition and its tension have determined both my destiny and my work."

Reinhold Niebuhr took the dialogical process yet another step. It is not just that we learn to operate on the boundary, he claimed, but that we have each foot firmly planted in quite divergent soils. He excited the imagination of the theological world with his insistence on the paradoxical as the appropriate way to understand the religious enterprise. Niebuhr argued that it is in the tension between polarities where God acts and Christian faithfulness takes place.

In more recent years, the dialectical method of doing theology has gone out of style. The fundamentalist right and the liberationist left seem to talk in categorical terms, without the ambiguity of the dialectic. There is little room for the either/or, let alone the both/and, in preaching that has inserted at the head of every point, "The Bible says." No one listening to a fundamentalist is left in doubt as to the absolute one-dimensional truth of everything. Nor do Gutierrez or Boff leave very many gray areas when they describe Christian social ethics.

We like to think of ourselves as creatures of the golden mean: "nothing in excess." It is written in our blood. To move to the extremes is a most uncomfortable exercise for most of us. It demands not only a sense of risk but a sense of humility, of not knowing, of hearing truth told from opposite sides of the room. It casts the believer onto the uncomfortable sea of the freedom of God, who may not be found in our theological absolutes; who holds the unjust under judgment, but whose love extends to the whole human family, not according to our merits but according to grace; who blesses the righteous, but whose rain falls on the righteous and the unrighteous alike; who loves the faithful, and who works through the faithless; who wants no one to be poor, and yet demands poverty of those who follow Christ.

We remain uncomfortable with important matters that are not solidly nailed down. The perpetual rise of fundamentalisms of all sorts is testimony to the fear with which we handle freedom. A generation ago, Erich Fromm, in his book *Escape from Freedom*, insisted that freedom is an intolerable idea for most of us, and that as soon as we are set loose from the chains of one kind of oppression we are in a state of panic until we find another tyrant or tyrannical idea to which we can submit ourselves.

What is true of individuals is also true of institutions. Those church bodies which are growing are those that hold the standards of orthodoxy firmly before their adherents. If a church can say, "Here is our creed, and this is exactly what it means," it has the inside track. If statistical success is our goal, then we must proceed without hesitation in that direction. On the other hand, those congregations which suggest that life is fraught with ambiguities, and that faith is lived on the boundary, tend to suffer from a statistical as well as a spiritual malaise. If one can point to clearly articulated positions, emanating either from a

Pope or a Bible, as the final infallible word of truth, the masses of people seem to feel comfortable. But to insist that growth and generativity can only happen in the tension between conflicting and in some cases opposite demands leaves many people in a state of gross dis-ease. It is, however, the very dis-ease that may point to our best hope!

And yet, as uncomfortable as it may be, the life of a faithful institution takes place at the edges. That is where God is most clearly encountered, decisions are made, and the Kingdom is evidenced. The easy way out of the struggle is to assume that growth takes place by mitigating, toning down, compromising radical alternatives. While truth is often found in the open space between competing ideas, the too-quick leap to the center often obviates the tension and thus diminishes the opportunity to seize the generative.

Throughout this book I will suggest that hope for the mainline church lies in the simultaneous commitment to widely divergent agendas. Our plea will not be for the toning down of opposing perspectives, but for sharpening them so that as they rub against one another, the vital is unearthed and the church is enabled to move forward. The alternative is that we set our compass on a course defined by the "successful" religious institutions of our era. I believe that course will only carry us onto the rocks of faithlessness.

Obviously little is to be gained by believing that the absurd is a legitimate pole of a dialectic. I am not pleading that we incorporate in our system those things we have solid reasons to believe are outside the will of God for our lives and the life our our churches.

In the succeeding chapters, we will examine a number of sets of defensible polarities before which the faithful congregation must live as we are confronted by the demands of God for our day. Hope for the mainline church may well lie in seizing both poles, and finding the fruits this more adventurous lifestyle inevitably produces.

2

Care and Courage

While this book is addressed to all those concerned about the future of the mainline church, it may have particular relevance to pastors or those in preparation for parish ministry. We need not catalog the chronic problems faced by mainline clergy. They have historically been underpaid, and their job descriptions impossibly varied. It is difficult to find a parish minister of any denomination who feels the placement system of his or her particular body is fair. They are often lonely. They are professional givers who have never learned how to receive—or have been taught that it is slightly sinful.

From time to time, ministers are threatened by issues beyond their congregations which have a striking effect on things at old First Church. A few years back a significant number of courageous pulpiteers took positions on the race issue, integrated their congregations, worked for passage of civil rights legislation, marched with Martin Luther King, and in the process unleased a whirlwind of hostility within their otherwise placid churches. Some retreated, promising never to mention race again. Others held fast and were summarily dismissed, or left in disgust. But others were able to weather the storm and have brought their churches along with them. More recently other issues have been the razor's edge many parish ministers have walked: disarmament, AIDS, creationism, homosexuality, abortion, unfair economic practices—to list but a few.

Clergy in denominations more congregationally organized often feel that they have the greatest problems. If a minister is called and dismissed by the parish being served, and there is no protection or even advocacy from the judicatory or denomination—no bishop or district superintendent who has authority—the clergyperson is often left to fight it out alone. Whatever the values, one would be hard put to find in the New Testament or in church history much support for the autonomy of the congregation. The word autonomy comes from two Greek roots meaning "law to oneself." It is difficult to see how any local body can be considered a law to itself. Ministers in such systems can be foully treated and nobody has the right to raise as much as a cautionary finger. What the congregation says goes, and that is the end of the matter. An assembly of bitter ex-pastors would fill a sizable stadium.

On the other hand, an occasional bishop may be more concerned about the peace of the church than its authenticity. In my experience, most shepherds of the wider church have been sensitive and helpful. Nevertheless, denominational protection is no guarantee that faithfulness to the gospel will be recognized and defended by anyone beyond the congregation. The malaise that affects parish clergy is no respecter of denominations. In the long run, the struggles that come with the territory in parish ministry will be fought out on a lonely battlefield where there is likely to be little help from any quarter.

A series of remedies have come into vogue, including the proliferation of clergy support groups, professional counseling services specifically directed to ministers, more tightly written contracts between pastors and congregations, and ministerial bodies that are almost unions.

Despite these safeguards, clergy-bashing still persists. Judicatory executives report that greater numbers of parish ministers are being driven from their posts by hostile congregations than they have seen in many years. Something is amiss. For whatever reasons, solid churches, as well as the perennial preacher killers, are engaged in the dismantling of well intentioned, adequately trained, and highly dedicated members of the clergy.

The problem underlying this pathology I believe to be theological, not sociological. We in the mainline churches—among both the clergy and the laity—are frightened, and the fear that has absorbed us is the fear of death. We look at the charts, examine the statistics, and see the waning of our strength. Futurists may debate whether the demise of the mainline church is inevitable, but our concern here is with how we live hopefully day by day within the structures we now have, while facing an unknown and unknowable tomorrow. It is the same question that every Christian must face.

There are frantic, faithless ways to respond to the fear of oblivion. Many who have, or think they have, terminal diseases seek quack cures, palliatives, and narcotics in an effort to fight off death and the pain that accompanies it. Substantial numbers of mainliners have frantically searched for quick fixes. In order to arrest the descent into oblivion, they do the American thing: They ask the pragmatic question, "What works?" The questions, "What is true?" or "What is the will of God?" are drowned out by the need for wonder drugs and pain killers. Churches that see only diminishing prospects look around to determine who has not been afflicted with the disease, and they attempt to mimic those they find in good health. Thus the basic theological question, "What is faithful?" is ignored in order to discover "What succeeds?" Success, in this case, almost always boils down to institutional strength—budgets, attendance, new members, buildings, and so on.

It is quickly discovered that flourishing churches share some specific characteristics. They are conservative theologically. They tend to take the Bible literally. They steer a wide berth around social issues that they have already determined to be unpopular in their communities or among their members. Many of these "successful" churches have moved in recent years from a position in which there was little discussion of any social issue to a position in which the social issues are carefully chosen to conform to prejudices already prevalent in the local culture. Peace and justice give way to personal morality—meaning sex.

I have long been bemused as to why in many churches war is usually acceptable and sex is usually wrong.

Led by notorious religious TV personalities, whose "shows" out-dazzle the entertainment most traditional parishes can provide, "gay-bashing" is in and disarmament is out. Homosexuality is universally evil and easily attacked.

Ministers in mainline churches have been tempted to mimic the popular styles of their more successful counterparts. We are a TV-oriented society. Significant numbers of people these days want to be perpetually amused. Many of us observed that what sells in our culture is entertainment—in short segments. We noted that numbers of those who entered our sanctuaries did not return because they told us they were bored by what went on. They had come to be made to feel good about themselves, and our ponderous styles suggested they had entered an alien, outdated world.

Mirroring what worked, we turned our sanctuaries into sound stages. We began to elicit applause at the "performances." We paraded across our "stages" the successful—celebrities whose individualism is impressive in a culture that worships at a shrine over whose altar is engraved, "We're number one!"

How has all this affected parish ministers? In scores of conversations and in correspondence, it is clear that there is much agony of spirit over the paths adopted by those who want to be faithful to the gospel but who find such faithfulness unproductive. Despite the frantic methods, their churches did not grow. They wondered if they were really doing ministry. They still looked with envy at the successful around them. While in many cases the dismal decline was arrested, something had gone out of the church that they found difficult to identify. And something had gone out of them as well. What they had lost en route was not only the gospel but also their courage!

Meanwhile the toxic side effects of the new drugs were beginning to be felt, and the contraindications were debilitating. A new malaise had settled over many of these frantic parish ministers. They had lost a sense of what they were really about. They had begun to abdicate their theological role, their prophetic and priestly functions, and they had become managers of institutions under the authority of theologically vapid boards of directors. They had done what they believed their laypeople wanted—and what their more secularly oriented laypeople wanted was institutional survival and success.

The current wave of clergy-bashing, of which we have spoken, seems to be happening in congregations whose ministers have attempted to salt their programs and styles with modest doses of wonder drugs gleaned from the shelves of the "successful." But the more they sought to satisfy their constituencies, the more irritable the congregations seemed to become. They, the ministers, discovered they were being grumbled against. When the murmuring persisted, many began to think about leaving their posts, and within a few months they had circulated the appropriate relocation papers or consulted with the judicatory officials responsible for placement. Many have left, either by their own decision or under pressure. While they were packing their books they scratched their heads wondering what had happened.

Near the top of my list of the world's most difficult middle-class jobs is manager of a country club. Few hold a position very long. They are regularly dismantled by their club's members. They can never please everybody, and those they don't please are perpetually on the warpath.

If there ever was a group called together on the basis of friendship and kinship networks, it is the average country-club set. The mission of a country club is to have enough of the right kind of members so that the greens can be kept in repair, the fairways watered, the swimming pool cleaned, and elegant meals served. The manager's job is to keep the members happy. If the club is not flourishing, if revenues are down, if not enough of the right kind of people are joining, and if there is grumbling among the established group which runs things, it won't be long until the manager is asked to leave.

While the manager of a country club may not ask appropriate theological questions, the parish minister must. What is the church really about? What is the imperative under which we operate? What is the relationship between the gospel and the powers and principalities of this present age? Why are we concerned about increasing the rolls of the congregation? What is the nature of the "success" we are driven to achieve? Is it simply a matter of institutional survival? Is evangelism nothing more than the reductionism of recruiting "our kind of people?" Or does evangelism have to do with rescuing the lost, converting the bigoted, training recruits in the art of turning swords into plowshares and spears into pruning hooks? Does not the fundamental mission of the church involve learning how to give the institution away, proclaiming a new order called "the kingdom of God," making the world a safer place for the hungry, the cold, and the marginalized?

In seizing one path to survival—adopting what works in contemporary culture—we have lost the tension of the dialectic by forgetting the other path. While we have taken church growth seriously, we have neglected the more basic task: Kingdom growth.

What is called for is a recovery of courage by those who have been ordained prophets, priests, pastors, and teachers. Having been drawn away from the authenticity of the gospel by sociological fears and dwindling statistical indices, many parish ministers now feel adrift, and a boat without a firm hand on the tiller will be the object of wind and waves and will eventually broach.

I am enchanted by the sea. As do others, I find it a regenerative experience to sail without the noise and smell of motors. Sailing is a pure experience. My batteries are recharged without discharging any mechanical gadget.

In the tidal waters off the coast of Maine, there are a variety of problems that keep sailors alert. In an area shot through with rocks and shoals, chart and compass are essential. If you know where you are and in what direction you are headed, most hazards can be avoided.

Reading a compass, however, is not a simple activity. There are two factors that can give a false reading. One is the metal in the boat itself. It will attract the compass and create a deviation of from one to five degrees. The more serious problem is the variation resulting from the northern latitude. Magnetic north is hundreds of miles from the north pole! Where we sail, that variation is presently eighteen degrees thirty minutes west. Not to be aware of the deviation is to risk running aground.

Perhaps the basic problem haunting mainline ministers and their congregations is magnetic variation. Success has become a false magnetic pole. They have lost their way. They are in hazardous waters. A generation ago we were much clearer about true north. Having come through the triumphalistic liberal era and having dealt with the profundities of neoorthodoxy, we had defined the nature and mission of the congregation and were convinced that our task was not to be successful, but to be faithful. Books such as *How the Church Can Minister to the World Without Losing Itself* (Langdon Gilkey), *Where in the World?* (Colin Williams), and *Call to Commitment* (Elizabeth O'Conner) encouraged us to think of evangelism as the broadest commission laid on the congregation. But it was an evangelism that had a social as well as a personal focus. Persons were called from bigotry, a trust in violence, and an individualism that thrived at the expense of the wretched of the earth, to become living evidences that the kingdom of God was taking root in the here and now. If God would bring in the kingdom fully, even then there were signs of its coming in the civil rights and peace movements, and later in the concern for the rights of women.

It was not an easy road to travel. Enormous courage was required. Many parish ministers found themselves in jail or dismissed from their pulpits. Thousands of laypersons also marched, witnessed, went to jail, and in other ways became living evidences of the purposes of God in history.

The church was a vital, life-giving agent of the kingdom of God. Perhaps nowhere was this clarity any greater than in black congregations, North and South. It was the black church that produced the civil rights movement. Martin Luther King, Jr. was a Baptist minister of a mid-sized congregation.

Mainline congregations and their ministers had a sense of identity. And if the compass and chart determined that they should sail through treacherous waters, they sailed, trusting the God of history.

But the foregoing is only half the story. If the clergy of that era were clear about the place of the gospel in the world, they were less clear about who they were as persons, pastors, parents, friends, husbands, or wives. They were people of considerable courage, but they were not, in the main, effective care givers. Many of them were absentee parents. They took care of the world but neglected their own families. Similarly, their congregations seldom saw them except on Sunday mornings when the sermon was sure to be about the day's most pressing social issue.

I speak from experience. During much of that era I was pastor of a thriving congregation in suburban Washington, D.C. As president of the Council of Churches of Greater Washington, I spent many more hours on Capitol Hill than in the hospitals, homes, and offices where the members of my congregation faced the problems that afflict persons one at a time. Sermons meticulously avoided personal issues. I had forgotten that any minister who stands in the pulpit looks out over a sea of broken hearts.

In the mid 60s I moved to a small but vital congregation on the campus of the University of Chicago. It was during the height of the student rebellion. When not involved with radical students, I was on the streets with members of black gangs. The war between the Devil's Disciples and the Blackstone Rangers was the most volatile situation I had ever encountered. Daily, hundreds of University students and street gang members pursued their quite different agendas in our church building.

After a night on the streets, sometime after 3:00 a.m., I was roused by the voice of a gang member who informed me that my church was on fire. While the structure of that great stone edifice was spared, the thick smoke left a heavy, web-like residue over every interior surface. As the sun rose I sat on the steps of my lovely building, crying.

Students, awakened by the sirens, appeared, determined to clean up the mess. By sunrise, gang members, alerted through their own mysterious communications network, also showed up to help. The congregation, whose annual meeting had been scheduled for that evening, was enormously understanding. It was a vital, committed group of people, but it deserved better from the pastor.

For years I had been oblivious to whatever personal problems members of the congregation might have experienced. I would make hospital visits if urged to do so. Beyond that I did little to share in the joys or the sorrows of the people to whom I was called as pastor. My own three children were almost as fully neglected. I was an absentee pastor and an absentee father. The church held together. The home did not. As my own sense of direction diminished, I eventually found myself out of the parish and engaged in the world as the chief operating officer of a modest corporation.

There was little variation in my theological compass. I knew where true north was. But if I was clear about the thrust of the gospel, I was less clear about the deviation that had developed in my own sense of ministry. And failing to compensate, I was off course.

Three years later I returned to the pastorate. I am still involved in the major issues that confront the world, now from the vantage point of a typical mainline, middle-class congregation. If there is a radical voice in our community, it has been mine. The pulpit puts the issues in "religionese." The more public statements and perceptions are put in "secularese." The message is the same. Only the language—the vehicle for the communication—is different.

However, the bulk of my time is committed to pastoral concerns. I carry a large counseling practice, make regular home calls, am in the hospitals almost every day, and am a full-time care giver.

I also spend more hours at home. I accept few dinner meetings, because that is the hour to be at my own table. Every three years I resign from every community activity I have accumulated and slowly decide what to take on.

When ministers write asking how I get away with what I do, I reply that I have decided to live in the tension of the dialectic between care and courage. I realize I may have what Mark Twain called "the calm confidence of a Christian—with four aces." The congregations I have served have been patient, forgiving, liberal, laced with laypersons who are committed to the mandate of gospel, and ready to love the earthen vessel sent as their pastor. They have been full of people who understand the relationship between care and courage and who not only permit me to live in the tension generated by these polarities, but live there as well.

As we identify the deviation in ourselves and the variation in the world, and correct our compasses accordingly, we will rediscover the roots of faithfulness and be the church we have been called to be. And God, who is faithful far beyond our definition of the term, gives the increase in the garden we plant, water, and tend.

3

The Pastoral and the Prophetic

The root pathology of the mainline church is the fear that continually narrows the scope of what it is about. Consider the way increasing numbers of congregations define their constituencies. While a few still see themselves totally dedicated to social reform, many more eschew that image and have narrowed their focus to taking care of their own. The following statements come from pastors of two quite different mainline parishes.

Pastor Jones: "It takes all kinds of churches to meet everybody's needs. I decided long ago I never could be all things to all people. I know my skills and my limitations. I'm not being critical of what anyone else does. I'm just telling you the borders I've put on the ministry of this congregation.

"My job is to make this the warmest, most congenial congregation in town. If you look around on Sunday morning you will see that we appeal to certain clearly defined constituencies. Many of our members are older, retired, and conservative. They've paid their dues. They want to be taken care of. When they are sick they want me present. I try to get to the home of every retired person at least twice a year—monthly if they are shut-ins. Their world tends to narrow as they grow older. They are not as flexible, not as concerned about what is beyond their immediate environment. I see no need to disturb them.

"Then there are the young families. We are one of the few churches in town that has both a large contingent of senior citizens and more kids than we have Sunday school rooms to put them in. Many of these families moved from the inner city because they feel safer here. Their children attend good schools. This is a low crime area. We have a homogenous population. People share the same lifestyles and interests. If we were to suggest that the church ought to represent some other point of view, most of these families would say, 'That's fine with us, but we are going somewhere else. We didn't come to this church to deal with the kind of people we moved to escape.'

"It is not that they are narrow-minded or bigoted. They just don't want the church to get involved in things that may make it tough on their kids. I think they deserve a place where they can associate with people who have common values.

"They go hard at it all week; right up against the tough issues of the world. They know how difficult it is to stay in business. When they pick up the newspaper or turn on the TV they are assaulted by all the troubles and problems of the world. They need to escape when they come to worship on Sunday, or when they engage in the other activities of the church during the week. Can't say as I blame them. Isn't religion about spiritual and interpersonal values after all? Don't we hear enough about disarmament, world hunger, and injustice every day, that we shouldn't have our faces rubbed in it when we come to worship God?

"If I got to talking about social problems I'd be out of my element. I don't know much about these larger issues. But what I do know convinces me it is a thin coin that doesn't have two sides. When our denomination passes a far-out resolution, and my people hear about it, they jump all over me and want to get our church out of the denomination. The best thing for us is to say as little as possible about what goes on in New York, whether you are talking about our denominational offices or the National Council of Churches.

"Look, I don't claim congregations that spend time and energy dealing with social issues are wrong, although in my opinion they seriously distort the Christian implication of the issues. That's just not our style. If you were to sum up what this congregation was about, you'd probably use words like 'faithful,' 'pastoral,' 'authentic.'"

Pastor Smith: "This is a prophetic church and people who come here know what we stand for! If that isn't where they are, they don't stay. Some time back I went through a crisis in faith. It was following a highly charged visitation campaign in which we were determined to add over one hundred persons to the congregation on one Sunday. We worked the plan down to the letter, just as we had been instructed to do by the evangelist who predicted how things would turn out. He was right. I stood in the pulpit that Sunday faced with a whole roomful of people who had come to join the church, many of whom I had never seen in my life. Instead of welcoming them individually I took them in like a recruiting officer inducting a new group of buck privates. 'Raise your right hand and repeat after me.' The three baptismal services that followed were more like dipping sheep than anything else. Never even called their names. Didn't know them.

"The next morning as I sat in my office, I broke down and cried. What had I done? What earthly relationship did all this have to the proclamation of the Kingdom? I was told that my task was to turn these new recruits into solid church members. I was to find out what their needs were, generate programs to meet those needs, and assure them they had ownership of significant portions of the church program. It was their job to tell me what they wanted, and my job to see they got it. What they wanted had little relationship to the gospel. They wanted a nice community club where they could be taken care of, their families entertained, and their prejudices reinforced.

"It took me six months to realize I could not be the chaplain of their club. I left that church and since then have sought to develop a congregation deeply committed to the social implications of the Christian faith. I think the agenda of the church in our day is clear: world peace and disarmament, the elimination of hunger and poverty, social justice, and saving the environment. Everything we do is filtered through these foci.

"We have carefully defined our constituency and the scope of our program. A lot of the Mickey Mouse most congregations get involved in never makes it through our front door. Every department is organized to deal with some aspect of the peace-justice agenda. My guess is that most middle-class congregations have drifted so far from authentic Christian faith they are unusable to God and dangerous to the human race. Look around. Religion is a big part of the problem. It is bigoted, self-righteous, and a haven for the pampered and overfed. It allows people to live with the luxury of never having to face the serious issues that confront the vast majority of human beings.

"This is not a club for the contented. In this congregation we are the advance guard of the Kingdom. We are a prophetic church. We don't pay much attention to solving personal problems. Instead we tell people to quit taking their own psychological pulses, and get into the world where they can do something that matters.

"We feed two hundred people a day—no questions asked. All they have to do is show up. We run a shelter for the homeless, a problem pregnancy clinic, a safe house for abused women. Our church is known as the peace information and action center of the community. We are a 'sanctuary' church for refugees from Latin America, have sponsored a nuclear freeze petition, and have declared the church building to be a nuclear free zone.

"You better believe we stay in hot water. Others in the community often say to our members, 'I hope you're not part of THAT church.' We're certainly not the most popular group in town, but why should we complain? We're a long way from having nails run through our hands and feet. All I have to take is a lot of verbal abuse. A couple of our young men went to jail a year or so ago because they were involved in a demonstration at a nearby missile site. The local press took them apart, but the congregation stood solidly behind them.

"We have lost several families in recent years. Our attendance and income are down. Some of the better-off older families couldn't take it. There are plenty of places in town for folk who don't want what we have to offer, but we will never soft-peddle the message for the sake of popularity. If you would sum up what this congregation is about you'd probably use words like 'faithful,' 'prophetic,' and 'authentic.'"

While a few churches can be characterized as being either purely prophetic or purely pastoral, most congregations occupy smaller and smaller territories somewhere in the middle. They do a bit of this and a bit of that—nothing at the extremes, mind you. Over their altars could be written the ancient dictum, ALL THINGS IN MODERATION. These congregations may harbor two remarkably different constituencies: those committed to a no-social-agenda agenda, and those committed to an all-social-agenda agenda. These two groups get along by ignoring each other. The institutional denial mechanisms are very strong. If one would encounter someone who doesn't believe the church should have anything to do with politics, for instance, and suggest that part of the program of the congregation does in fact center on these larger issues, you might hear: "Not really. The minister sometimes goes overboard, and there may be two or three members of the social action committee who talk about social issues, but very little political stuff is allowed to go on."

I have observed that argument even in congregations that are deeply committed to a prophetic agenda. Denial seems better than friction, and as long as congregants who would be offended by peace-justice issues keep that psychological mechanism in place, they have no reason to become alarmed at what they would consider an alien perspective.

On the other hand, I have seen church members clearly committed to social issues who assumed everyone else was just as committed. When the reality was pointed out, they refused to believe their congregation was not totally on the side of the angels—as they defined them.

In still other congregations there is a perpetual running battle between the two groups. For a period of time the prophetic enthusiasts are in control. They rise to positions of leadership, make certain their pastor agrees with them—or get a new pastor—and determine the public agenda of the congregation. The pastoral enthusiasts don't leave, they just go about their caring business privately, gathering strength until they manage to elect to positions of importance those who share their point of view. Budgets are then readjusted and the pastor either modifies her position or there is turmoil until she is called somewhere else, or decides to sell insurance. In no case does anyone dare suggest the congregation can and should do both things at the extremes. The result is a lack of vitality about anything, spiritual anemia, and slow decline. In the absence of the dialectic, little that is generative can take place.

Among those least successful in dealing with the pastoral-prophetic tension are leaders who talk largely in pastoral terms and try to satisfy the prophets by allowing a little study or engaging in a little rhetoric about social issues.

One pastor I knew thought every congregation should have a social action committee, but he also knew that his leading contributors would never allow even the discussion of controversial issues to take place. So he suggested the committee be called "The Social Committee." Its task was to plan the congregation's social events—parties, dinners, and entertainments. His hope was that having gotten the word "social" into the parish's vocabulary, larger issues could be addressed. They never were!

In a number of well-heeled congregations there is likely to be a significant amount of talk about social issues—rich churches also tend to be full of intellectually sophisticated people—but not much action. These churches may raise big bucks to feed hungry children in Africa, but when it is suggested that they examine their investment policies and divest themselves of stocks of corporations doing business with the apartheid government of South Africa, there is shock and amazement.

How does a congregation in an upper-middle-class, lily-white retirement village in the sun belt even become confronted with a socially significant agenda? It is far easier to spend its time leaning on Jesus, safe and secure from all alarms. The temptation is to define the church narrowly—a social club for the affluent with rather long invocations at its social events.

On the other hand, in an aggressive "liberal" congregation, whose leaders are committed to a social agenda, what happens to individual human needs that people legitimately have? If the minister is involved day and night with this peace action group and that hunger program, what happens to someone in the congregation who encounters a serious personal problem, or surgery, or the breakup of a marriage, or alcoholism, or the loss of a job, or any one of the hundreds of tragedies and crises people face? No matter what the makeup of the congregation, every minister preaches every week to a church full of broken hearts.

I know ministers who do no counseling, make no home visits, see someone in the hospital only when they are terminal, and are almost totally oblivious to what is going on in the lives of those to whom they have been called to minister. Several years ago I shared in a seminar with ten mainline ministers who were curious about how they could sharpen their counseling skills. In each of these congregations the fundamental agenda was the prophetic one. After the teacher had spent several weeks lecturing, he invited members of the class to present case studies and verbatim reports from their own counseling.

Of the ten, four admitted to having no active cases to present. They did not do any counseling—none! "Why?" they asked themselves. Could it have been there were no members of their congregations who had personal problems: no divorces, ungovernable teenagers, alcoholism, psychological knots, or even a single case of the bull-moose crazies? The chances are, these ministers had never seemed interested in what was going on in the lives of persons, never invited those in difficulty to come and talk, never got in a position where they might even know what was happening, and really had never cared. If it wasn't a peace and justice issue it never got their attention. Members who were faced with the common dilemmas of life either quietly dropped out, found support by using secular resources, or sat there and hurt!

There have been times in my own ministry when I was so caught up in saving the world I took no notice of individuals around me whose lives were going to hell. Like Pastor Smith, I knew what the church was all about. It had a prophetic message and mission, and if something came across my field of vision that didn't look like a social issue I never saw it. To live in a creative ambience is not to do a little of this and a little of that: to be prophetic enough to keep those who like and expect that kind of thing happy, and pastoral enough to keep those who like and expect that kind of thing happy. The faithful congregation does both without reservation, and it does them at the same time with the same people. While the temptation to define the mission of the church ever more narrowly is ubiquitous, hope for the mainline church lies in the opposite direction.

To narrow the gospel to one perspective or the other, or to put on the hair shirt of the prophet for people who want that and the backward collar of the priest for those who want that is not to be faithful, nor is it to be all things to all people. In the end it is to run the risk of being nothing much to anybody. And that is exactly what has happened in congregation after congregation. Reasons for the withering of the mainline church are clear to those who have examined its pale saltless style.

How are people to grow in the absence of the dialectic? The thesis of this book is that in the tension between polarities—in this case, the prophetic and the pastoral—growth takes places, the mainline congregation finds its hopeful agenda, Christ is encountered, and the vitality of the Christian enterprise is experienced.

During the days when the fishing fleets sailed from harbors along the New England coast, the second greatest problem encountered by sea captains was how to get the catch to port without spoilage. The greatest problem was how to get themselves, their crews, and their boats back in one piece.

Before the advent of refrigeration, the safest method for avoiding spoilage was to kill, clean, and salt down the catch at sea. But this was expensive and time consuming and severely strained the resources of the fishing fleets. As long as a captain could haul in a reasonable catch quickly and make it to port with healthy fish in the live holds, all was well. But if the ship was delayed by a storm or the volume of the haul, the fish would die and the entire catch could be spoiled.

The problem was even more severe when the catch was cod. That species slowly sank to the bottom of the live holds and smothered each other. One captain never seemed to have that problem. No matter how long he was at sea, or no matter how large the catch, his live holds never came to port with dead fish. Nobody ever knew why, and he kept his secret carefully guarded. It was not until the end of his life that he shared it with another captain—a gentleman who was not as closed mouth. It seems that before the miracle-working fisherman would put to sea, he would throw a few catfish into the live holds.

If you have dealt with catfish you realize that on their dorsal fins are very sharp spines. Catfish by nature dart along the bottom of the sea—or the live hold of a ship. When our good seafarer threw his cod into that hold and they would begin to sink to the bottom, pfft, pfft, pfft! they would be royally spiked by the catfish and would swim very quickly out of reach of that nasty spine, arriving back in port in robust health. At the same time, the catfish would be kept in motion by the descending cod. It was the encounter between catfish and cod that kept both alive.

Every congregation needs catfish, whose task it is to keep things stirred up. Just keeping things quiet is the path to the graveyard. We all know people who die ten years, or thirty, before they are buried. I do not refer to those who are seized with some debilitating physical disease, but those who stop thinking, growing, and struggling long before they are laid in the ground. They die because they are often protected from conflict by well-meaning, beloved pastors who believe their main task in life is to keep the peace. Entire congregations can sink into sleep, and finally death, in the absence of a vigorous dialectic.

Congregations also need cod, and lots of them! I once heard of a pastor of a strikingly liberal church who boasted that in all his forty years of ministry there was never a recalcitrant member or a church argument in his parish. It was later discovered that if a member surfaced whose opinion differed from the majority—and the pastor—he would be called into the study and presented his letter of transfer. That style of conflict resolution made for harmony, but it is unlikely it made for growth on anyone's part.

In later chapters we will discover how a sturdy dialogue can be maintained between these two widely divergent points of view in the same congregation and how that style of church life leads to health, spiritual vigor, and faithfulness to the gospel.

4

Jerusalem and the Ends of the Earth

Every congregation struggles with the relationship between the demands of local programs and ministries, and a commitment to the wider mission. Every faithful congregation does, that is. Hope for the mainline church rests in its commitment to a mission that begins where it is and extends to the ends of the earth.

But consider the stance of a mythical parish somewhere in the American Southwest. It is one of its denomination's largest churches. Its annual receipts exceed four million dollars—without a wide-ranging TV "marketing" mechanism. What money it gets it draws from its local constituents. This congregation has everything. Two organs and several grand pianos provide the background music for worship. The debt on its mammoth building, purchased from a congregation that constructed it but didn't have the resources to keep it fed, was paid off in two years. No stone is left unturned and no expenditure unappropriated in meeting the needs of the people who pour through its doors.

Year after year, hundreds take membership. The parish finds those most like the members it already has and brings them into the active life of smaller groups within the larger fellowship, thus welding them socially as well as religiously to the institution. It is a picture-perfect model of what church growth experts suggest we all can become.

If you were to drop in on any given Sunday morning, you would be moved by the music, the spirited worship of the people, and the power of the preaching. You might observe, however, that no mention would be made of any concern beyond the congregation. Nothing would be said about peace, race, sexism, or justice. Neither would South Africa, the Near East, nor any other troubled place be found among the concerns of that fellowship of faith.

Although an occasional offering might be taken for some personalized mission cause, the unjust social conditions found on the mission field would never be addressed. An analysis of giving patterns would reveal that although the congregation produces a remarkably high per capita figure for its local needs, the per capita figure for needs beyond itself is far below the median level of the denomination.

The anomaly is that most members of the congregation are only a generation from a debilitating social system. Looking around, one might observe they are no longer from socioeconomic underclasses. They are a newly monied group of folks, on the way up the social ladder, glad to be rid of the chains of bondage, and doing very well, thank you.

Two decades ago the minister was one of the clear voices for civil rights within his denomination. But he is no longer poor, or discriminated against, nor are his people.

An old friend, with whom he shared the hard battles of the 60s, once asked him why neither he nor his congregation had the slightest interest in any of the issues with which the wider church was struggling.

The answer: "Yes, I remember those tough days—the marches, the jails, the dogs and fire hoses. But we are not there any more; not me, not my people. We have escaped from all that; and good riddance. I know about South Africa, the poor in our own land, the grinding problems faced by those who have never escaped from discrimination. That is where my heart still is. But I've got to build up this church, make it strong enough to meet our needs. Why, this year we must construct three more parking lots. When we get our house in order, you can count on me to be back in the fight."

It could be fairly assumed that houses like that are never going to get in order. Three parking lots this year means a new building next year. And that means more staff, more promotional expense, more upkeep. It will take all the energy the congregation can muster to feed the dinosaur being created. That minister will never be back in the fight. He has mortgaged the congregation's soul. He lives with the delusion that the day will come when his institution will be in good enough order for him to lift his eyes beyond its doors.

There is no question but that his concerns, and those of his people, are genuine. Sizeable numbers are being "won," served, and inspired. But the congregation has now woven faithlessness into its fabric. There are paths that churches choose which, once taken, are impossible to turn back from. The point of no return has been passed when they say, "First, we've got to build up this church, make it strong enough to meet our needs. When we get our house in order, I'll be back in the fight."

This is not a new problem. One hears echoes from the time when the Hebrew people had become the kingdom of Israel—with all the problems attendant to keeping even a petty kingdom afloat on a troubled sea.

> When the LORD your God has brought you into the land that he swore to your ancestors, to Abraham, to Isaac, and to Jacob, to give you—a land with fine, large cities that you did not build, houses filled with all sorts of goods that you did not fill, hewn cisterns that you did not hew, vineyards and olive groves that you did not plant—and when you have eaten your fill, take care that you do not forget the LORD, who brought you out of the land of Egypt, out of the house of slavery. The LORD your God you shall fear; him you shall serve, and by his name alone you shall swear. Do not follow other gods, any of the gods of the peoples who are around you, because the LORD your God, who is present with you, is a jealous God. The anger of the LORD your God would be kindled against you and he would destroy you from the face of the earth.

When your children ask you in time to come, "What is the meaning of the decrees and the statutes and the ordinances that the LORD our god has commanded you?" then you shall say to your children, "We were Pharaoh's slaves in Egypt, but the LORD brought us out of Egypt with a mighty hand."

Deuteronomy 6: 10-15, 20-21

While our example of the large mythical parish may seem extreme, it is only a caricature of what goes on in many congregations. The board of First Church, Middletown, USA, is struggling with the budget for the next year. Projected revenues are just slightly higher than for the year just past. But this year the roof must be repaired, a new sound system installed, and the staff given a cost-of-living raise. Unless someone comes up with a way to increase income, something will have to be cut.

Inevitably a board member will articulate the sentiment others are feeling: "Well, we have no choice other than to cut our mission giving. We've got to take care of ourselves before we can take care of others. If this church goes down the drain there will be nothing to give to anybody. When we get things squared away here we can make up what we don't give this year."

The results of that course of action are predictable. Next year, instead of increasing the mission budget, the income picture will have further deteriorated, and the same dismal process will cycle around again. Without the tension inherent when a congregation pays simultaneous attention to local and world needs, everybody is let off the hook, and congregations off the hook don't do well. In the long run, faithlessness is the road to disaster—economic as well as spiritual. Any congregation whose concern ends at its city limits has already planted the seeds of its own death—first spiritual, and finally physical.

Consider what such a congregation has taught its members about family finances. One must take care of personal needs before one can consider any wider use of resources. There may be church members who manage to be faithful stewards out of their leftovers, but in four decades of ministry I have yet to encounter one.

It is not so much that a wider vision of the world is missing, but that within the congregation the dialectic, the tension, the struggle has been obviated by grasping the simplest alternative—limiting the focus of the congregation to Jerusalem and putting aside any concern with the ends of the earth.

An even more fundamental pathology is evidenced in congregations that pay scant attention to the ends of the earth because they are never informed. "I don't know enough to offer an intelligent opinion," comments the pastor. I have occasionally countered, "For God's sake, if you don't know enough about world hunger to make a clear statement, why not? Where have you been? What in the world do you suppose ministry is all about?"

The probabilities are that those reading this book understand the devastating consequences brought about by the pastor who uses his ignorance as a way to stay "non-controversial." If you don't know anything about an issue you are saved from having to discuss it, let alone take a position on it. This is particularly true in those congregations where the simplest stance on any concern beside abortion, prayers in the public schools, or pornography brands one at least a fellow traveler if not an outright communist. While liberal pastors in conservative parishes have special problems, they also have special opportunities to call people to rebirth.

But this book is about the necessity of the dialectic, and that means we have to examine the other side of the coin. While it is probably not as true in the 1990s as it was two decades before, there are still members of the clergy who are so caught up in social issues that they talk about little else.

People come to church with broken hearts, running wounds of body and spirit, and are not fed. The shepherd regularly describes, for the gathered sheep, the unjust way the pastureland is divided or the trouble in the sheepowners association. But bruised heads are not anointed with oil, rams caught in fences are never extricated, and lambs are never tended. The sheep come in hungry, tired, and hurt, and leave that way.

Often the sheep are not tended because a shepherd fascinated with the ends of the earth never stays in any one Jerusalem very long. Pity the sheep whose shepherd is perpetually on the lookout for another flock.

No one in any community where I have held a pastorate would have the slightest doubt about my social commitments. Indeed, in my early years of ministry that is all they heard. Over the years, however, my preaching has become more pastoral. If I started out playing a one-stop organ, as time goes on the number of voices has increased. Softer woodwinds are interwoven with trumpet calls.

Every Christian is automatically involved in the world's larger problems. If we all are crew on spaceship earth, every preacher must address, without hesitation, these issues. Not to do so would be faithless. But that is not the whole world, or even the primary world, of most of us. We live in a particular place, and we struggle with our own particular needs.

A few years back I was hospitalized with a terribly painful condition. Only a heavy narcotic managed to dull the agony. I was amazed at how small my world became. Pain reduced everything down to a tiny universe—about six cubic inches in my gut! I didn't want to read the newspaper, and I found that anyone intent on engaging me in conversation about a particular political problem in our community—a problem in which the week before I had been vitally interested—got a slight hearing and less response. There was only one thing I really cared about, could think about, and wanted to talk about—or be silent about, as was the case: my pain!

When any congregation gathers, it is a collection of broken hearts. More often than they hear them, these troubled folk need words of comfort, assurance, and hope. A family whose teenage son has just put a shotgun in his mouth and blown the top of his head off is not particularly excited about the need of the church to divest itself of stocks of South African corporations, or the way in which Christians are called to provide sanctuary for political refugees from Guatemala. But neither can the whole gospel be proclaimed without considering world hunger or the threat of nuclear war, as well as a plethora of other global matters.

It is a common misapprehension, in pulpit and pew alike, that to be faithful one must only deal with Jerusalem or one must only deal with the ends of the earth. The faithful congregation perpetually struggles in the midst of a dialectic, being stretched between quite dissimilar poles. It is in that struggle that faithfulness is born.

Consider yet another aspect of the dilemma. There have traditionally been great social pulpits and action-oriented congregations that can always be counted on to say and do something about disarmament, world hunger, and the wider global issues, but which are not particularly concerned about hungry children, slumlords, rape, and crimes of violence in their own communities. Care ought to be taken to insure that the issues which confront that local community, that Jerusalem, are adequately dealt with.

For a dozen years I was a political writer for our metropolitan newspaper. My picture and column regularly appeared on the editorial page. Early on I gave serious attention to the wider matters: violence, war and peace, world hunger, and the threat of nuclear oblivion. These issues were dealt with almost to the exclusion of what was going on in the city where the people who read that paper live. As the columns, and the columnist, developed more maturity—or should I say, faithfulness to the secular presentation of the gospel, which is how I define my political involvement—more attention was given to what was happening in city hall, at our local chamber of commerce, and at the county court house. In 1990 this concern for things local led me to engage more directly in public life. I ran for and was elected to the city council with enough votes to secure the position—but not enough to feel arrogant about it.

For a congregation to be involved in the global issues is risky business. If it is accused of mingling religion and politics, that accusation is no doubt correct. While the Constitution of the United States is clear about the wall of separation between church and state, the Christian gospel is equally clear about the absolute relationship between faith and politics. Any other posture is a reiteration of the docetic heresy—a gospel devoid of flesh and blood concerns, of incarnation.

While the discussion of wider issues inevitably yields great moral principles, the concerns that face Jerusalem are not so neatly categorized. To talk about a city council election, or how the sales tax is a blight on the poor, or why the closing of a school in the least advantaged part of town could be considered immoral, carries a tenuous theological burden of proof.

If I have gotten into trouble in the discussion of national issues, the trouble has been more direct when I have addressed local matters. Sooner or later one treads on the economic interests of live, very present individuals. Nevertheless, if the gospel has implications for the ends of the earth, those implications are just as operative for what goes on in Jerusalem.

While this discussion has thus far been limited to the polarities, Jerusalem—the ends of the earth, the biblical text setting the polarities includes two intermediate loci for witness: "But you will receive power when the Holy Spirit has come upon you; and you will be my witnesses in Jerusalem, in all Judea and Samaria, and to the ends of the earth" (Acts 1:8).

Faithful congregations find their mission in Judea and Samaria as well as in their own backyards and at the earth's most remote points. Indeed, these intermediate mission points may provide even more stimulating challenges to the imagination and thus to the vitality of mainline congregations.

It is not unreasonable to think of Judea as Nebraska, California, Missouri, or whatever state in which the congregation finds itself. The actions of the state legislature, the posture of the governor, and the decisions of the state supreme court are therefore well within the orbit of discourse and action for faithful congregations.

When state budget makers turn their backs on education, public assistance, and community development for the sake of buildings, highways, and bridges, the mission to Judea takes on new importance. In my state, Missouri, it is not difficult to discover what issues before the legislature have direct implications for faith and action. A network of sensitive Christians maintains an office at the capital. This politically sophisticated organization produces monthly reports which are available by subscription. Most states have similar watchdogs or lobbies.

Few public officials are more sensitive to the concerns of citizens than state legislators. If one good letter has influence with your congressional representative in Washington, chances are your state representative or senator is even more responsive to solid positions taken by those of his or her much more narrowly defined constituency. As more and more federal social programs are channeled through state agencies, increased attention will need to be paid to how funds and programs are handled at that level.

If the parallel between Judea and state government is defendable, what is the meaning of our mandate to be witnesses in Samaria? The Samaritans were outsiders, pariahs to the Jews, the disrespected cousins of Israel. Who where you live fits that description, and what is your mission to them?

In many communities the patterns of racial segregation are still as strong as they were prior to the civil rights days of the 60s. While schools within most communities are now integrated, in many cities the suburban white flight has created just another variation of a segregated educational system. Many municipalities are currently under court order to deal with that situation. Nevertheless, we still have two school systems in this nation, racially segregated and inherently unequal.

Beyond that, while industry, social clubs, golf associations, and practically every other aspect of American society have taken integration seriously, Sunday morning at eleven o'clock remains the most segregated hour of the week. There is a considerable volume of literature dealing with this issue, and it would be beyond the purpose of this book to examine how faithful congregations handle their own racial isolation, except to say that ignoring it is to be blatantly faithless.

Members of minority races and ethnic groups are not the only pariahs—Samaritans—in our society. Consider how mainline churches have often dealt with homosexuals. Homophobia is as pervasive in our day as was the fear of Samaritans when Jesus told a story in which one of these outcasts turned out to be the hero. The issue has been exacerbated by the AIDS epidemic, which is linked to homosexual activity. Ministry to Samaria in our era will focus on victims of AIDS. At this writing, society is unclear about how to react. The church has an opportunity to set the terms of that response.

Consider the following questions that faithful congregations must address: Is AIDS a divine punishment? What is the Christian response to the disease? What is the Christian response to those who have it?

First, is AIDS—or any disease, for that matter—God's punishment on sinful people (in this case, homosexual men, since homosexual women seem no more susceptible than heterosexuals so long as they stay away from bisexual men and dirty needles)?

In the Old Testament we often find a correlation between sin and suffering. Pharaoh disobeyed God and got boils. Lot's wife looked back and was turned into a pillar of salt. In prescientific days it was assumed that natural disasters were the results of sin. Some reason had to be found for crop failures and physical maladies.

But we are scientific New Testament people, and our hallmark is Jesus, who refused to blame disease either on God or on the sinfulness of diseased persons. A blind man was brought to him and the disciples asked, "Who sinned, this man or his parents?" Jesus sloughed the question. When they suggested that some foreigners on whom a tower had fallen must have been terribly evil, Jesus insisted that their unrighteousness had nothing to do with it. God did not send disease or tragedy as punishment.

Nor do we find Jesus condemning homosexuals. Social scientists tell us that the percentage of homosexuals varies little from age to age or from society to society. Affectionate relationships between persons of the same sex in Jesus' day must have been as prevalent as in our own. While he was profoundly concerned about sin, Jesus rarely alluded to the so-called sexual sins with which religion is often obsessed. His condemnations were reserved for the self-righteous, the unjust, those who thought they were better, purer, more holy than others, religious leaders who despised the poor and the weak, greedy farmers and businessmen, those who lived by the sword, those who assumed their piety would save them, those whose outer lives were clean but whose inner lives were full of hatred, bitterness, and prejudice. His harshest words were to those who believed persons not of their race or nation were less than human. But nowhere does Jesus castigate homosexuals.

While honest Christians differ as to the sinfulness of homosexuality, it is clear that actions have consequences, and certain physical activities are dangerous. Unsafe sex does, in fact, produce unwanted pregnancies, as well as a host of distressing and deadly diseases.

Second, what is the proper Christian response to the disease? What is the Christian response to *any* disease? We are first of all called to use common sense. Paul says that our bodies are temples of the Holy Spirit, and how we treat our bodies is a religious matter. Not to take care of the only bodies God has given us is contrary to God's will. Lack of exercise, overeating, destroying our lungs with cigarette smoke or our livers with alcohol, and wallowing in emotional tension (the root of many of our physical maladies) are contrary to God's will. If certain sexual activities produce deadly diseases, we had better stay away from them. Any sex ought to be safe sex. In the last analysis, the best protection from AIDS is a monogamous relationship which lasts more than five years.

A concern for Samaritans must include an examination of policies that keep Samaria in trouble. To be concerned about the AIDS epidemic means a change in national priorities. The faithful church will insist that tax money be spent for research to save us from dreaded diseases, and not for more weapons that have only one use: to kill great numbers of people quickly.

If we are serious about finding a cure for AIDS, or a way to protect people from the disease, we should be making a larger investment in research. The rising cost of medical care is not the issue if the health of the people is a priority.

During the plagues that ravaged Europe, it was the church that made the greatest single contribution to human survival in England: sewers! The insistence on a sewer system for London! Millions were saved because a few Christian leaders saw the construction of sewers to be the nation's number-one religious priority. If our bodies are temples of the Holy Spirit, a proper sewer system is indeed a spiritual issue. And so is AIDS research.

Third, what is the proper Christian response to victims of AIDS? Again we are driven back to Jesus. What was his response to the diseased and dying? It was never the disease that concerned him, but the person. Whoever the person was—the lame, the blind, the deaf—his focus was on that person, not on their pathology. "He had compassion on them."

Compassion is the only legitimate Christian response. The victims of AIDS are not ordinary sufferers. We fear them. We don't want to be around them. We don't want them in our buildings or our meeting rooms. We might catch what they've got, even though medical science tells us there are very few ways the disease is transmitted. Nevertheless, many would rather have these people live in isolation, in a separate community. Perhaps we should require them to dress in rags, wear bells around their necks, and cry "unclean" if we should approach them.

Not only are the victims of AIDS seen as Samaritans, they are leprous Samaritans! And Jesus was a friend of lepers. Despite their disease or how it was transmitted, Jesus violated the rules and the prejudices of the time. Lepers knew Jesus cared about them. He came to their homes and their colonies. He had compassion on them.

Other Samaritans in or near your gates may include the very poor, who are rarely excluded from our congregations but seldom made to feel at home. If they are accepted in the congregation's worship, what about the more intimate social circles that dominate our religious fellowships?

Congregations with a broad range of ministries find ways to include retarded or otherwise handicapped and disabled people. They make a special effort to welcome the blind and the deaf. They build wheelchair ramps. They seek out and welcome residents of group homes, persons trying to make it in society after being released from mental institutions, the emotionally troubled, and notable community misfits. (If you want to see otherwise dedicated Christians get nervous, listen to them after an agency has asked for a zoning variance in order to put a group home for former mental patients, delinquent young people, or the mentally retarded in a residential neighborhood.)

Not only is faithfulness contingent upon the full implementation of the mission of the church both in Jerusalem and the ends of the earth, but the places in between are important loci of mission as well. Christian bodies, as well as individuals, grow in faithfulness when they confront the difficult problems of competing spheres of missional activity and concern. While the argument can be made that it is problematic for any one congregation to be all things to all people, picking and choosing too carefully may only result in massive faithlessness. The faithful church lives on the boundary—one foot in Jerusalem, the other at the ends of the earth—and both hands in Judea and Samaria.

5

Being In and Of the World

Few admonitions are more difficult than that we should be in the world but not of it. The Bible rarely views the physical world as an evil place. It was created by God, loved enough for God to send a Son, and the locus of the Holy Spirit's salvific activity. "And behold, it was very good," was God's comment at the conclusion of creation. "God so loved the world..." rings out the New Testament's golden text.

When the natural world is referred to, the Greek word ordinarily used is "cosmos," denoting the created world, the world of God's beneficent productive activity.

In later canonical writings, and in some patristic texts, the world takes on a more sinister aspect. We see evidences of an anti-worldly docetism, with its distaste for all things fleshly, "worldly." The Greek word used in these more pejorative texts is usually a derivative of aion, meaning the present order, the natural condition, this age, the political system. It designates the way things work in society. It is this alien world Christ came to redeem.

If Christians live in the midst of less than benign political systems, we are nevertheless bound to another order: a world that is yet to come, but whose intimations we find presently realized in a company of faithful men and women—the church. It is for the coming of this new order on earth, as it is in heaven, that we plead in the Lord's prayer's central petition.

Christians are required to live in both worlds at once: the world of God's coming kingdom, and this present world—not only the present natural world, but the present political age. In its pure form, to live in the world but not to be of it may mean to escape to a monastery, or to develop some other communal system by which a religious body separates itself from the rest of society. Throughout history there have been experiments, few successful, which sought to extricate the faithful from this evil place. But if the Amish do not drive vehicles with internal combustion engines or wear buttons on their coats, and if Jehovah's Witnesses will not take blood transfusions or salute the flag, does that make them not "of" the world? It is easier to maintain an illusion of faithfulness to an anti-worldly command than it is to act it out authentically. There may have been a simpler era when families, and even small communities, could be self-sufficient, acting as if the rest of society did not exist. That time is long gone. We are both in the world and of it.

Of even less biblical sanction is the image that this world is such a rotten place that the only thing Christians can properly do is prepare for heaven. Thus the truly righteous tiptoe through this garbage heap holding their noses, trusting that at some point in their wretched journey Jesus will break through the clouds and carry them to their "real" home.

In conditions of poverty or slavery, those with no hope for release might be comforted with the thought that if they have little here they will have riches there. But that has more often been a counsel of despair foisted on them either by their masters, as a means of pacification, or, more compassionately, by the already defeated who saw them as hopeless fellow pilgrims, traveling through this barren land. Wherever the hope of the gospel has been manifest, there has been a call for action and a rediscovery of the liberating power and will of God right in the midst of a world under the control of the powers and principalities.

Among those who seem more enamored of heaven than earth, one does not tend to find a concomitant rejection of buildings, investments, TV studios, theme parks, and whatever else the coin of this realm will buy. Devout heaven seekers with whom I have done business on Monday may discuss the world to come but are attuned to the affairs of this one.

Most of us in mainline churches are certain the thrust of the Christian faith is not that we be taken out of this evil world but that the world be rescued, redeemed, and used in service of the coming reign of God. It is clear to us that this world, with all its warts, is the proper locus for God's redeeming work—and ours.

Certainly there is solid theological ground for such a conclusion. God loves this world and we are called to act out that love in history—in our history and in the place where we live.

Our question is not whether we shall live earthly or heavenly lives, but how we live authentically in the midst of the powers and principalities, the polluted systems and greed-ridden institutions which distort the creation and produce despair, hopelessness, and violence. It is not this world or the next, but whether this world shall continue to be under the domination of the old order or be invaded by the new. We live in both orders simultaneously.

We are compelled to take seriously the rules set down by the old order. But at the same time, we can never make peace with the kingdoms of this world. Christians are the precursors of a new order. We are the landing party of the new messianic age. To be faithful is to have both feet planted in the midst of this world, and at the same time to be the advance guard of the reign of God. We are to live fully and self-consciously in both worlds at once.

We now turn to specific ways in which this tension, this living in two worlds, affects the life of the faithful congregation. The dialectic is this: We are a haven, a refuge, an oasis, a sanctuary for the hurt and the troubled. But we are also the beachhead of the Kingdom, carved out on these inhospitable shores. We of the church are the reborn, the forward guard of God's invasion party, heralds of a new order. But there are also times when God's people need to be protected from the ravages of this present age. The church is also a refuge for those who come in from the storms of the world outside. It is an ark into which the hopeful and the faithful crowd. It is a front-line hospital for the wounded, the troubled, and the dying.

When I was a pastor in Washington, D.C., "Martin" was a member of our congregation. Martin was a member of Congress and a dedicated churchman, who took seriously the relationship between Christian faith and public policy. It took me a long time to see that Martin, like the rest of us, wrestled with his own personal demons and needed the church to maintain his sanity in what he saw to be an insane world. His social ethics were clear. He could be counted on to cast his vote consistently on the side of peace and justice.

Martin was chair of a powerful House subcommittee, which determined how money was to be allocated for higher education. He spent his life both in the world and of it.

Because such positions of responsibility are always lived out under incredible tension, Martin's personal life was troubled. His wife, who rarely saw him, finally left in despair. His two children were proud of him, but since he was an absentee father, they too abandoned him. Martin drank too much, took too little care of his health.

At this point a change was called for in his relationship to the church. He needed a place where he could withdraw from the world. He needed to get in touch with the spiritual disciplines: prayer, Bible study, the contemplative life, the witness of the Holy Spirit, "the peace which surpasses all understanding." While much of his public life was lived both in and of the world, he now hungered for the church to be a place where he could be separated from the world, where he could be not of it.

Martin joined a prayer group and engaged, with his pastor, in serious Bible study. For two years he refrained from addressing public issues in the church. He needed distance—room to work out his personal problems. The church became a sanctuary, a place apart. Martin's story is hardly unique; it encapsulates what many less public church members face day after day.

One rarely finds a congregation caught up in aggressive social action that also has room for the contemplative life, spiritual formation, piety, introspection, meditation, and "practicing the presence of God." There are good reasons why the mixture is difficult to come by. Nevertheless, the either/or, which seems to dominate the scope of most mainline congregations, fails to take into account the diverse needs of people in our communities of faith.

More often we tend to roll with the winds of culture, sometimes focusing on the inner life and sometimes on social ministries. That more reactive style does not allow the church self-consciously to decide what it shall do and be. Historic circumstances and cultural moods do the deciding. Although never immune from the tides which push society, congregations that assume a both/and and not an either/or posture are not so easily whipsawed.

Consider the dramatic changes that have taken place in parish styles in recent years. During the late 60s and early 70s I constituted the entire faculty in preaching and worship at a major American seminary. I was a part-time adjunct professor. My selection for this post was not the result of an academic search. I was only a handy community pastor. But I was all the faculty they needed, since few students were remotely interested in parish ministry. The focus was on vocations in the world, social action ministries. It was hoped that congregations could provide the funding for these ministries even though the recruits had little use for what parishes historically were about. Even conversations about prayer, the inner life, and the "still point in a turning world" were eschewed by these highly committed students. The world had to be rescued!

Within a decade, a new spirit began to invade mainline seminaries. Social action was out and personal development was in. That meant a renewed concern for the parish, not as a launching pad for social ministries but as a center for personal development. As a new breed of seminarians became pastors, the mood pervaded a significant number of congregations. If in the previous two decades parishes were focal points of radical social action, that phenomenon wilted under the more ego-oriented spirit of the nation at large.

What was going on in the theological community was the result of a broader change in the national temper. At the end of the Vietnam debacle, the United States seemed to withdraw to lick the wounds of war and to recover from the devastating trauma which had gripped the nation. We turned inward and became more concerned with nurture than with revolution or the plight of the poor that bred it.

Both the civil rights movement and the vigorous protest against the war had involved large numbers of both clergy and idealistic laypersons. But the serious ideologues were now showing signs of age, and by the end of the war most younger people no longer seemed drawn to these battles. There was, however, considerable new excitement being generated about the inner life.

Among non-theologically oriented college students the retreat from the hard social issues was also marked by a recommitment to academics, personal growth, and a secular kind of spiritual formation. Rooms filled with meditating students replaced rooms filled with political activists.

Because much of the heaviest anti-war activity took place in and around the University of Chicago, as pastor of an on-campus parish and chaplain to students, I had observed this metamorphosis up close. Our church building had served as the meeting place for a number of radical groups. It was the staging area for the student occupation of the administration building at the university. "A free store in a company town," we had dubbed it. The leaders of the infamous Weathermen were well known to us and at one point had attempted, without our permission, to use the church building as the embarkation point for the "days of rage." They were thwarted when friends of mine in the movement warned me about the violent tactics the Weathermen planned to employ.

Nevertheless, I was called before the grand jury, faced with FBI informers who had infiltrated organizations in the church, and accused of being part of a conspiracy. But the informants had grossly distorted the facts, and they were repudiated by other witnesses.

Chief among the leaders of the radicals was Rene Davis. He and six others came to be known as the Chicago Seven. The first time I saw Davis following the trial he was kneeling before the picture of a fourteen-year-old Indian lad, Guru Maharaji, who had parlayed a sizable quantity of pure hokum into a personal cult. "The Divine Light Mission" was the path Davis and a few others followed to get out of politics and into personal growth. Davis had severed his political ties to become the apostle of a teenager who had amassed considerable wealth in the process of becoming an incarnation of the deity.

What happened to Rene Davis happened to hundreds of other political activists. In short order, this swing in mood invaded many parishes. Where once they had to find sizeable auditoriums in which to hold meetings about world issues, now they needed little more than closets. Those of us who stayed on the front lines, where the battles were being fought with the powers and principalities, looked around to find that most of our friends were gone. They were off meditating, talking about the interior life, and "getting themselves together." Concern for the world had been transmuted into care of the self. Many congregations that could formerly be counted on to be on the cutting edge were nowhere to be seen.

The loneliness was devastating. Is it any wonder that we took such a dim view of the "spiritual disciplines"? To us they looked like cop-outs. Individualism seemed antithetical to social reformation, and concern for the ethics of the Kingdom took a diminished place in the lives of our younger colleagues. We felt abandoned. The pendulum had swung entirely too far to the right. But that was the direction in which American society had already moved. To the extent that the church is a reflection of its culture, the change in the shape of the religious enterprise should have been expected.

If at one time I might have insisted the pendulum be forcefully pulled back, I am not now at all certain that is the appropriate response. The thesis of this book is that only as we pay close attention to both sides of the coin, both extremes, and engage in polar disciplines simultaneously, will faithfulness result and a new synthesis become possible.

While I maintain a healthy skepticism about the validity of the cults that flowered in the wake of the radical movement, I now see the quest for spirituality as vital to Christian experience. I am not calling for equilibrium, some rehearsal of a golden mean, but for the command, "Full speed ahead in both directions!" Only in the tension that this command generates will anything new and salvific come about in the life of the church and the world. If the mainline church is adrift, the root cause may be its failure to live antiphonally.

There will be tension in any congregation that is committed simultaneously to a radical social ministry and to the cure of souls, but that tension is redemptive, not destructive. Indeed, faithfulness demands congregations do both, vigorously and with the same people. The church is called to be in the world and of it.

Faithful churches are planted in this world. They must deal with the conditions established by the powers and principalities, whose almost cosmic influence grinds away at the human spirit. But that is only half the story. While faithful churches and their constituents are committed to this world, they also must pay attention to those who are beaten down by this world and those who cry out for a place away from, not of, this world.

This means that we build caring communities, prayer groups, healing ministries for the cure of souls. It means that every congregation needs to develop a relationship with a retreat facility, perhaps in a monastic setting, where Christians can sit at the feet of spiritual masters and have the wounds inflicted by the world bound up.

The tension lies in living fully in both worlds at the same time. It is not that we live with one foot in each. It is not that the new order is a Sunday world and the old order a weekday world. To divide life like that is to be half alive to each, and a heresy. One rather lives under the tension of being rooted fully in both worlds. We do not withdraw from the old order to be part of the new. We do not try to resolve the tension. We live in the midst of the tension. The hope of the mainline church is to be up to its neck in political involvement and social reformation, and at the same time to be a center for the cure of souls and the flowering of the spirit.

6

Church Growth and a Radical Faith

Two profoundly different evangelistic agendas confront mainline congregations. Both are implicit in the scriptures. We are first commissioned to bring into God's fold the lost sheep—to rescue the perishing, call to wholeness those who are broken, and provide for these new Christians a community of faith. We are therefore directed to build up the church, care for the institution, extend it, make it strong enough to perform its mission in the world.

The church is not a throwaway, another disposable bit of plastic. It has substantial and permanent value. Few of us would want to live in a community without churches. Calling people to the life and work of the church is not a peripheral matter. Institutions that fail to replenish their ranks die. Building up the church as God adds to it "those who are being saved" is central to the Christian enterprise. We properly call that endeavor "evangelism."

On the other hand, the church does not exist for its own sake. Its purpose is not defined by its survival. The care and feeding of itself is not its central mission. It exists to give itself away. It never puts its own needs ahead of the needs of the world—of the least, the last, and the lost. It exists to serve, even at the cost of its own life. That self-giving mission in the world is also properly called "evangelism."

Church growth/the radical posture in which the church is willing to lose itself for the sake of the world: these seemingly opposite enterprises define the church's evangelistic task. It is not a question of doing one or the other. The faithful church does both.

Mainline parishes are having a tough time seeing how these twin evangelistic modalities work together. The temptation is to forget the second for the sake of the first. In an effort to build up the church in an era when memberships are declining, we have been tempted to dilute the gospel for the sake of church growth. When it comes to a choice between what it sees as self-preservation and the enormous needs beyond itself, congregations only rarely rise above institutional chauvinism. We need not belabor how the instinct for self-preservation works itself out in the typical parish.

How many times has the following speech been made in boards, sessions, or vestries? "If we are going to pay our bills we had better go out and get new members. This church is dying on the vine. Many of us are getting old. Where are the energetic workers to replace us? And what about young people? Aren't they the church of the future?"

The problem is complicated by a lust, deeply rooted in the American psyche, for growth, success, more this year than last year. If the charts don't properly ascend, the spirit of the people slowly descends. And a failure of spirit is the first sign of institutional death. Nevertheless, when we become more concerned about institutional preservation than we are about the wholeness of persons and the world in which they live, we are in danger of idolatry. The church does not exist for itself. It exists for God and for God's world.

At this writing, the debate between the advocates of church growth and the advocates of a radical social understanding of the gospel continues to rage. In my previous book, *A Guide to Liberation Theology for Middle-Class Congregations* (CBP Press, 1986), I described the pitfalls of "church growth." Reactions were predictable.

One correspondent replied: "You may sneer at the church-growth movement, but how will you serve the needs of the world once you have allowed the church to shrivel to nothing? Are you willing to give it all over to the fundamentalists? How can you maintain a witness to peace and justice, to feeding the hungry and challenging the powers and principalities, if you have no home base left?"

The argument sounds compelling. Since the publication of that book in 1986, the statistical condition of mainline churches has not improved. Indices continue to show a marked deterioration in almost every category.

While the current debate has focused on issues that are largely pragmatic—what works—underneath is a larger theological question. Does, in fact, a radical religious perspective, which puts the wholeness of the world ahead of the survival of the institutional church, insure the diminution and even the death of the latter? Does a concern for the society inhibit personal evangelism? Does social action militate against church growth?

Let us assume, for the purposes of discussion, that a commitment to a radical, socially oriented acting out of the gospel does imply a serious trade-off. Loyalty to social reformation, let alone social revolution, may well militate against the strengthening of mainline denominations and their congregations. While it may be argued that the two concerns are only loosely tied together and that there is only a correlative rather than causative relationship, a substantial body of data shows that the growth of the institution stands in inverse relationship to the commitment of that institution to a radical social ethic.

The case was first made by Dean M. Kelley in 1972 in *Why Conservative Churches Are Growing*. Although those who already harbored suspicions about the leftward drift of mainline denominations jumped at the thesis as a reason to discount social witness, Kelley was not implying the automatic converse of his title. He was not saying that liberal churches shrink because of their social witness. He rather argued that conservative churches grow because they generate loyalty to their institutions liberals seldom develop. They expect high levels of commitment. They insist their constituents maintain rigid standards of behavior, stewardship, and religious practice. Mainline churches make no such demands. It is not the social ethic that distinguishes conservative growing churches from liberal shrinking ones but the quality of dedication expected. Kelley held that when nothing much is required, nothing much goes on!

Liberal churches were on the skids because they were offering a product nobody was calling for in an age in which the proliferation of available institutions—secular as well as religious—put little premium on voluntary societies that expect little and demand less. By definition, religion is a discipline, and without discipline religious institutions tend to be effete. It must be remembered that Kelley is a friend of the liberal establishment, not its foe. His book was descriptive, not prescriptive.

Ever since its publication, Kelley's book has been dug out and quoted in defense of a perspective that assumes social action is tantamount to willing the death of the institutional church. Despite disclaimers that he had intended to show a direct relationship between the social agenda of an institution and its ability to grow, he failed to explain why those two emphases were so consistently in conflict.

In most mainline denominations there are now groups of more conservative clergy and laypeople who are attempting to move these churches away from their roles as advocates for social transformation. They do so on two grounds. First, they argue that pronouncements of church assemblies do not speak for the parishes of the denominations. If congregations voted on the issues that come before denominational conventions and boards, the results would be quite different. Church leaders tend to be far more liberal than the constituencies they represent. That is the nature of theological leadership. The apostles never called for a referendum on whether gentiles should be welcomed into the churches of Asia Minor, and when the apostolic decree was read in the congregations dominated by Judaizers there was, no doubt, considerable negative reaction.

The second and more substantial reason is their ideological disagreement with positions the larger church has tended to take. Politics, churchly as well as secular, involves the ability to count, and the conservatives are tired of losing. If I never win a tennis match I will conclude that tennis is not a game worth playing. I may even try to turn the tennis courts into lawn bowling pitches, a game at which I am more adept. One suspects that many conservatives are weary of being in the minority.

My denomination, the Christian Church (Disciples of Christ), has a long record of positions taken on a broad range of social issues. In recent years there has been a concerted effort by a vigorous minority to move us away from advocacy. The loudest argument has been the insistence that churches long on social action are short on church growth.

Statistical evidence has been produced that "proves" that growing churches are either silent about social issues or take a considerably different stance than positions espoused both by mainline denominations and by the National and World Councils of Churches. One only needs look at the Southern Baptists, Assemblies of God, Missouri-Synod Lutherans, Latter-Day Saints, and Jehovah's Witnesses to ascertain that there is at least a correlation between statistical growth and the soft-pedaling of "liberal" social causes.

Since few conservatives want to appear to stand in opposition to social justice or world peace, the case has often been put this way: "The question is not whether the denomination has been wrong in its pronouncements, but whether any stance or activity should be countenanced that sidetracks the church from personal evangelism." If conservative Christians make the point on theological grounds, church growth enthusiasts take the position that any social posture is institutionally counterproductive.

Many church growth advocates also hold that the ecumenical bent of mainline denominations is detrimental to upbuilding the institutional church. The same sort of statistical data is adduced which indicate that denominations either involved in mergers or discussing them are shrinking, while denominations committed to the correctness of their own positions, over against the rest of the Christian world, are growing.

Writing in *The Disciple*, the national magazine of the Christian Church (Disciples of Christ), a leading church growth expert insists that mergers between two congregations may not be counterproductive, and that mergers between denominations from the same family tree—two groups of Lutherans, for instance—is acceptable. But mergers among denominations of diverse backgrounds violate a fundamental principle of church growth. The writer maintains,

> Christian unity is a great and right ideal, but we run a great risk when we put it higher on our priority list than Jesus put it in his. He prayed that "they may all be one" in his famous prayer at the Last Supper. But he only mentions unity this one time in the entire New Testament record. Five times in that same prayer Jesus expresses his basic purpose—"that the world may believe" (Herb Miller, *The Disciple*, February, 1985, p. 53).

Miller seems to mean by "that the world may believe" the commitment of individuals to specific religious institutions, a somewhat restrictive interpretation of Jesus' statement.

Since the same denominations that tend to have a social action agenda are also deeply involved in union conversations, church growth advocates are naturally suspicious of structural ecumenicity. They would include in their caveat participation in the Consultation on Church Union (COCU), as well as involvement in the work of the National and World Councils of Churches.

The suspicion that conversations about merger dilute loyalty is close to Kelley's intended thesis. He says, "Such ecumenical endeavors may be conducive to brotherhood, peace, justice, freedom and compassion, but they are not conducive to conserving or increasing the social strength of the religious groups involved or—more important—the efficacy of the ultimate meaning which they bear" (*Why Conservative Churches Are Growing*, Harper & Row, 1972, p. 175).

If growth occurs only in those bodies that call for serious commitment to their sectarian particularities, is evangelism compromised by ecumenicity? Advocates of church growth strategies insist that the strengthening of denominational loyalties builds, while their weakening diminishes the evangelistic witness. Put bluntly, the question is this: Must we retreat into sectarianism in order to maintain the strength of the institutional church?

The stance assumed throughout this book is that such thinking is a trap. Contrary to the position taken by those who advocate a pullback from the ecumenical movement in the name of institutional survival, I would argue that the only way to move ahead is to do social action AND personal evangelism simultaneously without one compromising the other; further, that the commitment to church union must go forward simultaneously with the concern for individual conversion. If our dialectical understanding of history is accurate, then we admit, apriori, that there is indeed vigorous healthy conflict between church growth techniques and a commitment to social action and to the ecumenical movement. But the conflict is ultimately the path to institutional health!

At this writing, the vigor of mainline, ecumenically oriented churches has been seriously eroded. There is a surly spirit abroad. In the United States, "successful" religion tends to be nationalistic and constrictive. For those churches committed to social transformation and ecumenicity it is a disheartening time, what Kelley calls "an adverse era."

Ours is not the decade of liberal religion. That time died with the end of the Vietnam War. It may never be resurrected in the way we experienced it in earlier years. Yet, in due time I predict the tide will turn, and we will see a resurgence of strength in the traditions and practices of mainline, middle-class congregations. If that be the case, we need to keep them as healthy as we can so that we will be prepared to sail when again the waters flood in among the rocks, covering the dry shoals and moving us out into the deep. However, we must also be prepared for a totally new thing that God may bring to pass.

To be frightened out of our faithfulness on pragmatic grounds—"Making pronouncements or taking action on social issues militates against institutional success," or "Talking about denominational mergers is not conducive to church growth"— is to be servants of the wrong gods. The popular deity called success is seductive in the extreme. We are not called to be successful, we are called to be faithful, and making decisions only on pragmatic grounds may be remarkably unfaithful. Indeed, faithfulness is our only hope—our only path to survival.

Let us return, briefly, to Dean Kelley. While it is easy to take the wrong message from his book, to misuse the data—to believe he suggested that faithfulness means giving up social action and ecumenical concern—Kelley dropped a few important clues as to how mainline churches might behave while the times are out of joint.

He describes how growing churches share a number of important characteristics. He lists: clearly articulated goals, the kind of controls that call for loyalty and commitment, and the capacity to articulate the beliefs and standards that members are required to adopt. In the final pages of his book he lists five rules for "Conserving Strength in an Adverse Era":

- Be in no haste to admit members.
- Test the readiness and preparation of would-be members.
- Require continuing faithfulness.
- Bear one another up in small groups.
- Do not yield control to outsiders, nor seek to accommodate to their expectations (p.176).

Far from backing away from our ethical and ecumenical agendas, it might be better to pay attention to Kelley's rubrics. We can become clearer than we have been for a long time about the radical implications of the gospel, the meaning of commitment to Christ and Christ's work, the expectations faith places on those who would respond to it, and the seriousness with which any prospective member must take on the mantle of the Christian faith.

Perhaps church growth techniques will turn out to be short-lived, easy answers to difficult problems—and that means no answers at all. Kelley's model is far removed from going out and finding "our kind of people," convincing them they are among their own and soft-pedaling the radical demands of the Christian enterprise so that they remain perfectly comfortable in our ranks, even if unchallenged.

Having offered the cautionary word about the direction in which the church growth movement seems to be taking us, let us now turn the coin over and discuss how faithfulness implies a serious commitment to the health of the institution. What are the positive things that church growth can teach us?

Church growth reminds us that in every community there is a natural constituency that mainline churches need to identify, invite, and welcome. In many communities, liberal churches may have the largest untouched body of prospective members of any religious institution in town. I can only tell you the story of one congregation.

The city in which I live is a conservative community of seventy-five thousand, set in the northwest corner of Missouri, the "Show Me" state. St. Joseph is fifty miles and fifty years from Kansas City. It is dominated by an insular mind set, which traditionally has not only been unwilling but seems unable to look beyond its restrictive borders. Its largest, most aggressive churches are fundamentalist tabernacles and congregations of denominations known for their conservatism. The question is often asked, "How can a liberal congregation committed to ecumenicity and social action make it in such a community?"

As long as we put the question that way, we continued to die. Since the community was conservative and what was left of the congregation was not, there was little we could do but talk about the good old days. It was not until we took a serious look at church growth, appointed a church growth task force, allocated a significant sum of money to tell our story, defined our target population, and re-allocated staff responsibilities that we made an amazing discovery. The largest unchurched group in town was not made up of nascent fundamentalists waiting for just the right tabernacle to root them from their closets, but disillusioned liberals who had dropped out of a multiplicity of churches when wave after wave of conservatism had washed over them.

These people had become convinced that the church was not interested or concerned about what went on in society, was filled with superstition, treated the Bible as a collection of magic texts, was dead wrong on every social issue, was engaged in sectarian reductionism, was anti-scientific and anti-Semitic. Having come to believe that was what the modern Christian movement was all about, they did the only intelligent thing they could. They jumped off the left side of the church into secularism, and they had been adrift for years. They are not the yet-to-be Christians but the no-longer Christians. They became our target group, and we developed ways to call them back to faith.

While still not a mammoth congregation, the church is now stronger than it has been in decades, even if it continues to suffer from an increasing set of negative sociological and geographical problems. It has a huge old building in a downtown that has practically been abandoned. Not only has the business community moved to the suburbs but physicians and other support facilities are also largely gone. Urban renewal did not stem the tide. It simply exacerbated problems already present. If there was ever a demographic description of what makes a dying religious institution, we had all the characteristics. It was only as we identified a natural constituency, got our message to them, provided small groups in which they could develop ownership of the church's program, and built loyalty to what we are about, that the congregation was turned from death to life.

We did not abandon our social and ecumenical agendas, instead we gave them new impetus and visibility. We have been the focal point of the nuclear freeze movement, and the center for the creation of a political block that redirected the city government and scored eight for eight in the election of a new city council.

It is possible for a liberal church to sit on its corner and die. It is happening all over the country. An institution, as well as a person, can die to the glory of God. But liberal mainline churches are passing away not to the glory of God but only because they have failed to be involved in an internal dialectic. A radical faith coupled to a church growth methodology has given at least one congregation a new hope and a brighter future.

7

Two Flags—Two Loyalties

As in most churches, ours has two prominently displayed flags. On one side of the nave, below the chancel, stands the Christian flag. Opposite it is the flag of the United States. These flags are periodically the subject of a modest internal debate.

Occasionally someone will remember that the flag code determines how banners are to be displayed in a public place, and ours are wrong! According to the code, when they are on the platform, the American flag stands to the speaker's right, the place of honor. When they are on the level of the audience, the American flag stands on the right side of the auditorium, again the place of honor. Our placement tends to be just the opposite, although the young people who carry banners in our processions often forget which flag goes where. Few are aware of the flag code and fewer think it is an important matter. But when the issue is raised by someone for whom the American flag is a symbol of life or death—more often a military veteran—the argument for appropriate placement is either made with some vigor, or the advocate quietly repositions the flags.

That action inevitably produces an equal and opposite reaction, and the minister will receive a call: "Pastor, the flags are wrong again. In the church no national flag takes the place of honor. We are a community with a loyalty above any national loyalty." Sooner or later we can expect the caller quietly to reset the banners, and the cycle will begin again.

Since there are always those around for whom conflict is uncomfortable, someone will comment, "Why have any flags? The national flag has no place, and the Christian flag has little meaning. To remove the flags would settle the argument." Or would it?

We set aside the debate on Pentecost when flags from many nations are displayed, symbolizing the universality of the church and the multiplicity of tongues that accompanied its birth. When folk see the flag of the Soviet Union and the flag of the United States side by side, at least the level of consciousness, if not of anxiety, is raised.

Our decision has been to leave the two major flags in place and use the resulting discussion to remind ourselves that we live in a political jurisdiction and in a non-political jurisdiction. When we enter the church we do not leave the world with its other important loyalties. When we reenter the secular world we do not leave the church. We are residents of both no matter on which turf we happen to be at any given moment. As with the other polarities we have discussed, this issue is not finally resolved by choosing one alternative or the other, but by living in the tension and allowing the dialectic to determine and shape the new and the salvific.

There is, however, a complicating factor. Our nation is currently being swept by a new wave of nationalism, which has engulfed many religious institutions and used them for political purposes. One often wonders where fundamentalism leaves off and national chauvinism begins.

With the rise of communism, certain defenders of the faith have also become defenders of the American way of life. By that they mean free enterprise and western values. The Christian message is thereby trapped in the ethos of the state. America becomes "Christian America." There is a renewed effort to put prayer and Bible reading—Christian prayers and Christian Bible reading, to be sure—back in the public schools.

The greater the perceived external threat, the more the political structure sees the importance of mobilizing and using religion as a tool of national policy. The Reagan administration played that game and played it hard. The first president in many years to rarely darken the door of a church became the symbol of a Christian, anti-Communist crusade. One needs to know little about history to sense the danger of that swing to the right—politically and religiously.

A case in point comes from an era not that long past. With the collapse of Kaiser Wilhelm in 1918, a new German government was put in place, the Weimar Republic. It was a democracy styled after our American system. Every man and woman was given the right to vote. The common people were offered, at least theoretically, access to the wealth of the great industrialists and landowners who had previously controlled the German economy. The military leaders, who were at the same time the giant landholders, or Junkers, lost their enormous power not only because of the new democratic emphasis but because Germany was disarmed. Many of these industrial giants had made their fortunes selling armaments to the government.

Under the terms of the Treaty of Versailles, the German army was to become subservient to the civilian establishment. It was President Wilson's hope that the foregoing war would end all wars and finally make the world safe for democracy. A neutralized Germany was the key to his hope. The Weimar Republic did not work. The Junkers refused to cooperate with it for obvious reasons, and there was no other substantial base on which to rebuild a viable economy. To the East, communism under Lenin and later Stalin was on the march. Not only did the Russians have designs on the Balkans and Eastern Europe, but there was considerable Marxist support in Germany itself.

The Treaty of Versailles also called for war reparations from Germany to be paid in gold, thus depleting what modest economic resource the nation had left. Inflation was rampant. At the end of the war, in 1918, it took seventeen Deutsche marks to buy a dollar. In 1931 it took trillions! People were paid twice a day, just to keep wages up with inflation.

Into the vacuum flowed a series of small political parties. Among them was the National Workers Party, later to be called the National Socialist German Workers Party, or Nazis. Their rhetoric was violently anti-Communist. Their political platform fit the dreams of the Junkers, and in short order the cry went up: "We must build arms!"

These political right-wingers picked up support from those who were fearful of all things liberal, such as a more relaxed sexual ethic, the breakdown of the traditional family in which the male ruled as king, and the proliferation of what they felt to be unsavory and unchristian literature. Attempts were made to reinforce the old family structures and to censor printed materials. On May 10, 1933, six months before Hitler came to power, there was a mammoth bonfire in Berlin. Thousands of books were taken from the libraries, schools, and universities and burned, many of them classics.

Sensing both the power and the limitations of his Nazi party, Hitler began to cast about for a universally popular movement through which he could solidify his gains and rally the nation. He found it. On May 23, 1933, he said, "The party stands for positive Christianity." Hitler had discovered his ally. It was to be the conservative German church. Later he said, "The Christian faith will safeguard the souls of the German people." In the previous year, he had begun to mobilize the German Protestant clergy into what came to be called "the German Christian Faith Movement."

Many of the Roman Catholic clergy were appalled at this turn of events. The more liberal wing of the Catholic church had formed a society called "Catholic Action." When Hitler came to power he outlawed Catholic Action, and on June 30, 1934, its leader, Fr. Erich Klauseman, was assassinated.

By the time Hitler was appointed chancellor, a full third of the Germany clergy had joined him, including a former submarine captain turned pastor, Martin Niemoeller. Another third of the clergy refused to join what became known as "the Conservative Revolution." Later there were mass arrests, and sizeable numbers of these Christians were executed. The other third didn't believe politics and religion had any relationship. They were only interested in personal piety and a religion devoid of social implications. Almost all of these innocents ended up in Hitler's corner, believing that a good Christian should support the government. Hadn't St. Paul said so?

Among those who resisted the Conservative Revolution were Christians who formed an underground church. They were led by Niemoeller and Dietrich Bonhoeffer, both of whom had become disillusioned with Hitler and believed Germany's only hope was to overthrow him.

There was yet another way Hitler used the church. The slaughter of the Jews did not start all at once. The Holocaust came on slowly and insidiously. It began almost innocently. An Englishman, Richard Chamberlin, had written a book that "proved" Jesus was not a Jew but an Aryan. The Conservative Revolution saw in it the justification for an anti-Semitism, long held in much of the Germanic church, and began to talk about a Christian Germany, free from Jewish influence. Lists of Christian merchants were advertised in the popular press. "Buy Christian" was the theme. Who were the non-Christian merchants? The Jews of course. Thus began the persecution.

The culmination of this identification of Christianity with the cause of the Third Reich came on November 13, 1933, just a few days before Hitler was appointed chancellor. A great religious rally was held in Berlin, and from it came the slogan that was to be the rallying cry of the new order: "Ein Volk, Ein Reich, Ein Glaube!" "One people, one government, one faith!"

According to Hermann Rauschning, a close friend of Hitler and one-time president of the Danzig Senate, "In no other nation was the clergy so servile to the political authority of the state." Rauschning coined the phrase, "the Conservative Revolution."

Who suffered? Confessional Christians; six million Jews; intellectuals; the handicapped; free thinkers; those with a different lifestyle, called gypsies; homosexuals; liberals—and the rest of the world. If all started innocently. Slowly the church identified the interests of the gospel with German nationalism, and gradually the gospel was lost.

Centuries before, Pope Urban II, after consultation with the political and mercantile leaders of Europe, agreed that the church would be used to reopen the trade routes to the riches to the East, and along the way to recapture the Christian shrines from the infidels. In 1096 he preached a sermon in which he declared, "Deus wult!" "God wills it!" Thus perhaps the most immoral and bloody chapter of Christian history was written. Why anyone today would call a religious effort a "crusade," given the sordid nature of the original episode, is a mystery.

The issue is not what happened in Nazi Germany but what commonalities can be seen with a more contemporary historical analysis. A facile parallel cannot be drawn between the way Hitler used the church and what is happening in contemporary America. I recite this bit of history only as a cautionary tale. There are good reasons for our insistence on the separation of church and state. We are now seeing government all too ready to use the religious right for its own nationalistic purposes, and if we are frightened by that turn of events, there is sufficient reason.

The easy answer is to see the government as the enemy of the faithful church. In fact, there are those who hold a devil theory of political authority. But the American government is not the enemy—at least not yet. Nor is honest patriotism somehow beneath genuine Christian commitment.

We are citizens of a proud and good nation. There is much to be thankful for. The Constitution of the United States is perhaps the noblest political document ever penned. It begins, "We the people...." A system, with all its warts, that rests on government of, for, and by the people may be the finest experiment in the capacity of a people to rule themselves ever devised. The system guarantees freedoms and opportunities. We have the right of protest, of saying "No" to the demands of the state when they conflict with the demands of God and of conscience. To be pro-God does not mean we must be anti-American.

Perhaps we have given away too many good words and good ideas to those who use them ignobly. I like the word "evangelical," for instance. And there are fundamentals that are of the essence of the faith. I also count myself a patriot, and I believe in the efficacy of this gracious land in which I was born.

We will leave both flags in our sanctuary. They remind us of who we are: simultaneously citizens of a proud and prosperous nation, which is both glorious and terribly sinful; citizens of a divine kingdom, which demands our absolute allegiance. In the struggle that tension produces, we may find a better way into the future.

8

A Sending and a Receiving Church

Many of us reared in mainline congregations cut our teeth on a passion for world missions. The congregation I knew was often visited by missionaries from remote corners of the earth: Africa, India, Japan. I remember being transfixed by stories these saints would tell about their work, and the world to which we had sent them, a world I believed no one else in the congregation would ever see. The globe was much larger then.

The missionaries never appeared without a trunk full of artifacts, which demonstrated how different that world was. The people who inhabited those dark jungles wore peculiar clothes, or no clothes at all. We saw pictures of "natives" of the first sort, but we had to rely on *National Geographic* for the second.

The rationale behind our mission work was clear. We were taking the light to those living in the darkness of paganism. We had a story to tell to the nations, which would turn their hearts to the Lord. We had the gospel and they needed it. We were the providers of mission, and they the recipients. Our role as sending churches has been a major part of the identity of our middle-class, mainline congregations. The vitality of the North American church depended on its missionary outreach. "Preach the gospel to every creature," was the final command Christ left with the church. We were a people under orders. No one foresaw that this commission could be subject to alteration.

Mission work was more than preaching. Inherent in the great commission were other human values. We built and sustained hospitals, clinics, and dispensaries. We constructed and staffed schools for precious little ones, who otherwise would live in ignorance, as well as sin. We provided agricultural experts, well diggers, engineers, and a host of other technicians whose task it was to translate the gospel into food, sanitation, and safety.

Not only was our parish visited by a variety of heroes for Christ, but we raised money each year for our own "living link" who provided the bridge between our flock in Philadelphia and an eye clinic in India. To an impressionable child, Dr. Victor Rambo was up there with the Trinity—and far more accessible. As things heated up prior to World War II, he appeared one evening with two large boxes, one filled with medical supplies, and the other with gas masks. "Which shall I take back to India?" he asked the hushed audience. For one small child the peace of the world, as well as the salvation of souls, became inextricably mingled with foreign missions.

Summer conference was the focal point for recruiting young people for "full-time Christian service." Our sturdy youth group often would make the yearly pilgrimage to a tiny junior college where with those from other congregations we would spend a week immersed in prayer, study, fun, and the consideration of what we were going to do with our lives. During the final night's consecration service, decisions would be publicly declared. It was obvious that our friends who opted for foreign missions were the most dedicated. As we stood in a circle, those choosing Christian education—always young women—would take one step forward. Those who had been called to the pastoral ministry would take two steps. But those committing their lives to the foreign mission field would take three steps!

Two members of my high school class took three steps and were commissioned by the congregation to carry the gospel to the ends of the earth. A few years later, now educated and married, they went to what had been called the Belgian Congo and was then known as "The Congo," where they served as medical missionaries. By the time the nation became known as Zaire, the hospital where they had worked was operated by Zairian Christians.

A crack in the system occurred three years out of seminary when I came across a young Nigerian pastor who was completing his theological education in the United States and had been assigned to serve one of our black congregations in the Nation's Capital. Late one night he recited the following story:

"My grandfather was the witch doctor of our tribe. One day white businessmen arrived in our village. They wanted our land and our gold. We would not let them have it. With them came missionaries who wanted our souls. They put a book in our hands, the Bible, and taught us to bow our heads, close our eyes and pray. We did. When we opened our eyes our gold was gone and our land was gone. But we still had the book, and now the day is coming when we will be returning it to you. We will be the missionaries and you will be the 'natives.'"

I did not then understand what this grandson of a witch doctor was talking about. But in his arrogance he left a mark on the still impressionable heart of a young American pastor. What might it mean for the gospel to be returned to us? Three decades later the meaning is coming clear.

A generation ago it became obvious that our highly successful endeavors had spawned a multiplicity of autonomous churches, neither dependent on us nor obliged to carry our sectarian banners. Indeed, they had little use for the divisions we had foisted on them. They had names like The Church of South India, The Church of Zaire, The Church of Japan.

Instead of sending them missionaries, who lived in compounds and whose task it was to westernize as well as Christianize the "natives," we were now engaged in a partnership, helping them do what they wanted and needed done and responding to their requests instead of taking them what we thought they ought to have. The term "missionary" gave way to "fraternal worker." Now our overseas staff worked for them, under the direction of indigenous leaders. We no longer had mission churches. They had become mission partners.

History does not stand still, and we are about to enter a new era with new rules, a new dynamic, and a dramatically new theological perspective. The new winds are described in the seminal work of Walbert Bühlmann, a German Catholic theologian who once headed the wide-ranging Capuchin missions. In *The Church of the Future* (Orbis Books, 1986), Bühlmann traces the history of the missionary enterprise in the Catholic tradition, and then he projects its future. He describes how the church increasingly finds its strength in the Third World. He asserts that the first thousand years of church history were essentially Eastern in theology, world vision, philosophic structure, and mission, and that the second thousand years—the millennium we are about to complete—has been dominated by the Western church and its philosophic presuppositions. This Western church, basically European, has in latter years become heavily North Americanized. His assertion is that the third millennium will be dominated by the Third World church.

At the beginning of the present millennium, 85 percent of all Christians lived in the West. But by the year 2000, two-thirds of all Christians and four-fifths of humanity will live in Africa, Latin America, and Asia. Already there are more Christians in Latin America than in any other of the six inhabited continents. The sheer weight of evangelized populations is now dramatically transferring the power of the Christian movement from Europe and the United States to the Third World.

Although the enormous concentration of populations residing in Asia dramatically affects percentages, even larger numbers of our Christian brothers and sisters can now be identified as living in the region stretching from India to Japan. We can no longer talk about a benevolent people taking the gospel to nations where the church is so weak it has no significance apart from the involvement of the sending body. Former mission churches are now developing a sense of their own missionary outreach.

With the rise of the church in former mission lands, the deterioration of the churches of the West continues. Europe and North America may be Christian in name, but their real religion is now secularism. Thousands of congregations in North America now include on their roles more inactive than active members.

And in Europe the great preponderance of baptized Christians have no visible relationship to their parishes. Millions of names are still registered on church documents only out of respect for family tradition.

Given the scope of the change in demographics and the ecclesial reality of the world scene, Bühlmann suggests that the focus of evangelization will rapidly shift from the "not yet Christians" to the "no longer Christians." We will become the objects of the missionary enterprise in the third millennium, not its subjects.

The implications are staggering. Western Christians are already in a minority. What is more, as the weight of numbers has dramatically swung to the Third World, so has the weight of vigor, power, and witness. The most generative churches are those in places we formerly considered our mission lands.

We have been used to thinking of our place in the missionary enterprise as the sending churches. While it may be premature to think of ourselves only as receiving churches, although that day may come, there is another way to view the data. Bühlmann suggests that we must begin to think not about sending and receiving nations, but about the mission of the whole church on six continents.

The fundamental question, we must remember, is not institutional survival but the proclamation that "the kingdom of God is at hand." It is the radical transformation of human society that is called for, not new strength for our ecclesiastical establishments. It is the liberation of the oppressed that is the heart of the evangel, not the preservation of mission boards.

Thus the new missional dialectic: For the foreseeable future we will be both sending and receiving churches. The thesis we have pursued through this book is that hope and new life come as we learn to do quite different things with full energy at the same time. If our analysis is accurate, the question before us, as we face the task of world mission in the twenty-first century, is how the giving and receiving will be shaped.

Since this book is primarily addressed to mainline congregations, the vantage point from which we will examine the issue at hand is the life and work of the parish. Since I have spent my ministry in congregations, I am predisposed to think of ecclesiological matters from that perspective.

The methodology I suggest is a substantially biblical notion later borrowed and revised by Karl Marx:

From each according to resources.
To each according to needs.

What is it that each church has to give? What is it that each church needs to receive? What gifts and graces will we in the West still have to offer? What will be our emerging needs that can be most appropriately addressed by others? Since we are more immediately comfortable with seeing our role as sending churches, let us begin by cataloging the resources we have that others may be able to use.

Unless there is a marked change in economics, we will still control most of the world's wealth. Looking far down the road, that situation might be considerably altered. There are those who hold that sometime in the next century, substantial economic and political power will reside in nations of the southern hemisphere. For the foreseeable future, however, we in the North will continue to control the world's goods, services, capital, and scientific know-how. The Third World will remain poor. Whatever else is given and received, the Third World will rely on us to fund it.

Permit an example from the life of the congregation I serve. For three years, 1983-1986, we had in our midst a couple from Indonesia who came to us as "missionaries" from the Christian Evangelical Church of Minahasa. It was impossible for the church in Indonesia to fund this mission effort; therefore it was funded by our denomination's mission board with some modest support from the congregation.

In the midst of this venture I had the occasion to meet with Dr. Willie Roeroe, president of the Indonesian church from which our "missionaries" came. He cited a number of reasons why his church was interested in this new relationship. First, there was the obvious need for his pastors to enlarge their experience by being in aggressive Western congregations. He was also enthused about the ecumenical implications in which his church would be directly related to a denomination of a different background and culture. These were the ostensible reasons for the project.

But underneath was an even more compelling rationale. If the Christian community in Minahasa was to be fully a church, even though it had long since ceased to be only a mission of the Dutch body from which it sprang, it had to act like a church, not like a mission. And that meant it had to send missionaries as well as receive them.

The Third World will no longer be content with meeting our needs to fulfill the great commission. Their similar needs are now coming into focus. Most of these Third World churches cannot now handle the enormous financial commitment it takes to do overseas work. But that is not an impossible obstacle. In our case a partnership was developed in which the church in Indonesia could become a sending body and we could help finance the venture, as well as being the recipients of its missionary zeal and witness. While it might be argued that there were more appropriate places for the Indonesian church to send fraternal workers than a middle-class congregation in an affluent American city, the arrangement into which we entered met a number of important needs for both that church and its North American partner.

In the long run we would hope that the financial burden of missions on six continents could be shared by churches in every place, but for the time being that part of the task must be borne by the churches that control the wealth.

Contrary to what we hear from political leaders, the need of the world is not for capitalism but for capital! That means the 7 percent of us who control more than 40 percent of the world's resources must learn how to provide the funds without demanding the sole right to determine how they are distributed.

At the same time, we must do what we can to redirect economic and political systems that keep others in penury and subservience. If this rich and powerful nation experiences a conversion so that "justice rolls down like water," the rest of the world might receive the best gift we have to offer. As Dom Helder Camera said to a group of visiting North Americans: "If you really want to help us, go back to your own country and work to change the policies of your government that exploit our country and keep our people so poor."

There is obviously much beyond our wealth that we have to share: longtime workers who can serve as spiritual midwives, interpreters, bridges; persons with special technical skills; our natural good will and enthusiasm; a growing sense that we see ourselves as part of a worldwide community of faith; our capacity for compassion; personnel willing to do short-term specific ministries in strategic places where host churches identify special needs. Our congregations may learn how to be recruitment centers for retired people with particular skills, as well as for young people who have a sense of calling to overseas work without some of the no-longer-useful missionary impulses. These are but a few of our gifts and graces for which the world hungers.

We now turn to the more compelling problem: how to view ourselves as receiving churches. What is it that the emerging churches in what we used to call "mission lands" have to offer us? How do we understand ourselves as sharing in missionary partnerships by becoming receivers as well as givers? I mention four, each of which deserves book-length treatment: a revitalized sense of liturgy and celebration, a recovery of Christian spirituality, a new theology of action, and new models of congregational life.

Liturgy: While much of the Western liturgical tradition is profoundly rich, in our mainline, middle-class congregations there is a growing suspicion that the words are there but the Spirit has departed. We have a form of religion without its power. Western liturgy grew out of a cosmology that no longer holds. Nor do we still operate with the Greek world view in which substance and accidence are easily separated. A generation ago we learned from Rudolf Bultmann about demythologizing both scripture and theology. Perhaps the church in Africa can help us demythologize, de-Westernize, the liturgy.

Worship in the African church grows out of the ground, the natural world. Walbert Bühlmann puts it this way. "For too many Westerners a 'proper' mass is one read from the printed page....They ought to go to Kinshasa where the liturgy lasts up to two hours, where the participants, young and old, fully take part in praying and singing, with gestures and swaying of the body—a drama, the weekly festive witness of the people." (*The Church of the Future*, Orbis Books, 1986, p. 98).

The African church may offer us the gift of finding a relationship with the earth again in liturgical forms that relates the body and the spirit; the human community and the natural world. (A further discussion of a revitalized Christian worship will be the subject of chapter nine.)

Spirituality: Less than a generation ago a significant number of young people, suffering from the spiritual aridity of Western life, rediscovered Eastern religion. Many of us put them down, called what they had encountered a fad—an escape or a cult—and wrote them off. But our spiritual aridity still exists. The churches of Asia may help us re-dig the deep wells of the spirit. In this way we may discover the Christ who is to be found in non-Christian religions of the East. It is not an amalgam, some false syntheses, that we seek—not a syncretic blending of Hinduism, Buddhism, and Islam with our experience. We do not foresee the immediate emergence of one big happy world religion. But the Eastern churches, planted in the same spiritual soil in which these other religions have flourished, may have discovered a part of God's truth that we have misplaced or never known.

A theology of action: Liberation theology is more than a Christian aberration, more than a wedding of Marxism with the needs of the poor. The implications of orthopraxis over against orthodoxy are enormous. A fuller discussion of this topic will be presented in chapter ten.

New models of congregational life: Vital new forms of parish life have emerged throughout Latin America. These house churches—known variously as the church of the poor, basic Christian communities, base churches, or the peoples' church—offer fresh models which may be the most important contribution to us from the Third World Christian experience. We will return to this subject in some greater length in chapter ten, where the discussion will turn to the dialectic relationship between new and old forms of congregational life and organization.

Global mission in the twenty-first century can become an exciting, life-giving encounter in which we learn to receive as well as give. Perhaps our salvation will come as we find the mission of the whole church on six continents, and we are encountered by the Spirit of God who has much for us to learn at the hands of our brothers and sisters in "One great partnership of love/Throughout the whole wide earth."

All the projections concerning the church that we have detailed in this chapter need to be seen in a wider perspective. If I read the winds of history accurately, not only will the beginning of the new millennium mark a quantum change in the role of the church, as the locus of power and authority moves from north to south, but the same shift in the geo-political sphere seems inevitable.

If the last thousand years have been dominated by Europe and more lately North America, it is increasingly clear that Asia, Africa, and Latin America will play dominant roles during the next period of human history. As of 1986 the United States became a debtor nation. One only has to look at the industrial and technological dynamism of Japan to sense in what direction the winds are blowing. And if we think Japan to be a serious competitor, just wait until China, with its billion citizens, mobilizes its resources and applies the classical Chinese intellectual power to them.

Already we are bearing the marks of a client state. Many of our manufactured products are no longer able to compete on the world market. Instead we are exporting raw materials and food, and importing finished goods. Thus we have assumed the role of the more primitive economic power, while others have become the leaders in the developed world.

Even if we do not choose to become a receiving nation in terms of religious traditions, we are already well on the way in the commercial sphere. Since God is a God of history as well as nature, this geo-political shift will have enormous theological implications. The faithful church will see the opportunity as the occasion to learn and to grow from the wisdom and vitality of a new world on the move.

9

A Recovery of the Sacred

No matter how far-ranging the program of a congregation might be, its center is found in what happens when the community gathers to proclaim the Word and receive the sacramental signs of grace. A failure of spirit among mainline churches has come about as they (1) perceive they have lost their focus in worship, (2) become confused about what the liturgy should or should not contain, (3) don't know how to match the competitors—religious and secular—who increasingly encroach on our formerly sacred time, and (4) long for the emotive in what they sense to be a sterile and all too rational liturgical environment. Hope for the mainline church involves a refocusing of its central liturgical act.

First, the perceived loss of focus: As is the case with most of the issues we have thus far addressed, the root problem is theological. A people who are no longer clear about the God they serve will not be certain how to celebrate the presence of that God in their midst. With the disappearance of God from the skies and the demise of the notion that God is the male leader of a patriarchal cult, the focus of worship was blurred. The issue was compounded by a cultural obsession with entertainment, so that worship became a way for God's spokespersons to amuse, and thus control, the audience. Contributing to the malaise was the loss of the biblical notion of priesthood. As these factors coalesced, it was little wonder that liturgy turned fuzzy.

How do we approach the Holy when we are no longer certain of the holiness of anything? How do we bow before the Mystery when we believe we can resolve life's most important mysteries in our laboratories and think tanks? In this increasingly known and thus smaller world, there is little Mystery—the inscrutable unknowable authority which is not ours to fathom. There are only problems. And problems can be solved with enough time, smarts, and money.

It is not that God has recently disappeared from the heavens—we passed that turn in the road a generation ago—but that God has disappeared from the profundities of life as well. If worship is the adoration of and submission to the Mystery we call God, and there is no Mystery, what becomes of worship? It is reduced either to an anachronistic exercise for those who have lost their religion but can't quite break the habit of going to church, or it becomes little more than an effort to ritualize the nature of our human relationships and our need for community.

Congregations must again become centers of theological inquiry. We seem so concerned with programs, the "how," that we may have lost sight of the "why." Pastors are resident theologians. When that role is obviated for the sake of being the tour director, program manager, or business agent, it is little wonder that the congregation's theological grasp is fuzzy. Every minister is a theologian, despite protestations to the contrary. The question is whether she will be an adequate theologian or an ecclesiastical mechanic who keeps the ship running without much attention to its direction.

Years ago in the slums of industrial cities, there was an epidemic of lead poisonings affecting young children. The children were eating flakes of paint that had fallen from long-neglected walls. It was only later discovered why these children were consuming such vast quantities of tasteless paint chips. Their diets were deficient in nutrients, particularly minerals, and their bodies were compensating by ingesting whatever minerals were available—in this case, lead. The wisdom of the body determined that minerals were needed but seemed unable to discriminate between what was poison and what was not.

Most heresies are not deliberate efforts to move outside orthodoxy—"right doctrine," or, more specifically, "right praise"—but are rather attempts to compensate for an essential theological ingredient missing from the spiritual diet. The current wave of fundamentalism flooded in when God disappeared from the heavens of mainline religious communities and faith became only a horizontal and relational phenomenon. Having lost the Mystery, a basic human hunger was met by eating paint off the walls—poison flakes of biblical inerrancy, magic, judgmentalism, nationalism, "Jesusism," and individualism. The electronic revolution spread the disease almost instantaneously. For those of us in mainline churches, to address the theological issues that produced these distortions, by ingesting even small doses of the same poisons, is not only dangerous but also faithless.

The recovery of focus in the liturgy involves confronting the Mystery again—this time in terms of depth, not height. It would be equally as heretical to attempt to shove God back into the sky. Nevertheless, the depth of the unfathomable human encounter with the Holy is the only corrective. Once the focus of worship is clarified, issues of content are more easily addressed.

Having lost the focus, a second problem arose: How should the liturgy be shaped? What materials and ceremonies should it contain? When the church I serve in Missouri was built in 1917, its sanctuary featured a pulpit-centered stage. The minister was backed by a choir in elevated rows. The communion table was a bit larger than a card table and sat four feet below the foot of the pulpit. While the rationale was to have it on the same level as the people, in reality the pulpit-centered nature of the liturgy made any other placement architecturally difficult.

Early in the 50s, as neoorthodox and ecumenical emphases were in the ascendancy, the room was redecorated. The chancel was divided. A large altar now dominated center stage, and choir members were moved to the sides facing each other. They were to assist in worship, not to perform. To tone down Sister Smith's red hat and Brother Jones' paisley tie, the singers were uniformly robed. Candles flanked the altar with appropriately garbed acolytes to service them. Renovations of this sort occurred in hundreds of mainline churches.

Styles in music also changed. Every church that had made do with a piano now had to have an organ. The advent of electronic instruments simplified the problem, although the thirst for a *real* organ was never satisfied until pipes appeared. Hymnals that included a generous selection of gospel music—what the folks tended to call "the old hymns"—were replaced by service books with "better" music, theology, and poetry.

Chancels began to take on the colors of the liturgical season. Banners sprouted like mushrooms. The clergy, who had been in tails and striped trousers, now were turned out in academic gowns and stoles. The service itself became more "formal."

Eventually the ecumenical emphasis, through the work of the Consultation on Church Union (COCU), produced a common liturgy. Large numbers of mainline congregations used or adapted this "high-church" form. With the advent of common lectionaries, the liturgical distance between the churches dwindled until one could rove from congregation to congregation and not know the denomination without looking at the name on the church's signboard. The World Council of Churches' classic document of the mid 80s, *Baptism, Eucharist, and Ministry*, summed up the finest theological foundation for the liturgical revival, drawing the major denominations and churches of the world even closer together.

Each of these modifications was a step forward. The problem was that almost every one of the denominations, whose leaders were enthusiastic about the reformation of worship, was shrinking, some at staggering rates. If the services were now properly arted and liturgically correct, the sanctuaries where they took place were increasingly empty. Those churches, however, which had moved in exactly the opposite directions were experiencing enormous growth. It took no more than a sideways glance to determine they were doing something right, if the goal was to fill their auditoriums—the word "sanctuary" being anathema.

Mainline church leaders began to inquire as to what they might do to capture a share of the success that their less formal neighbors were enjoying. If worship was to be a bit longer on the entertainment of the pious and a bit shorter on the proclamation of the Word and the celebration of the sacraments, what forms and artifacts were permissible?

What worked was obvious. First, every service had to be dominated by the resident superstar, who was both the MC and the PR voice of the institution. He also had to speak with no uncertain tongue—unless it was a heavenly tongue. His word was law, because it had been directly revealed to him from God—through the scriptures, of course. Doctrine was simple, direct, and without question: no either/or. There was no allowing the congregation to consider various ways to understand the faith, no posing a question that was not answered. There were no imponderables—and hence, no Mystery.

Architecture had to be rearranged—again! Having the holy table at the center had to go. Split chancels were a fad in most reformed traditions, after all. They came into vogue only when we quit calling Roman Catholics nasty names and started falling all over ourselves to be more like them. If they took on the vernacular, we, at least, could get the Eucharist back into the center of the liturgical experience.

Emotional appeals were essential. The purpose of singing the same refrains and choruses over and over again was to manipulate the feelings of the congregants. One also had to update the music. Bach was out and Bill Gaither was in. Theology not only had to be simple, it had to rest on a verbally inspired, authoritative scriptural record whose key verses were easily quoted and remembered.

Not that we were at all prepared to adopt these modifications wholesale. The secret would be in injecting just enough of them into the bloodstream to reap their advantages without catching the diseases they carried. Having asked the wrong question, "What will fill our buildings?" there was no way we could arrive at a correct answer. Had we rather asked, "What is authentic worship?" we might have been able to entertain a number of fresh and powerful ideas, which would have, as a by-product, reinvigorated not only what we did, but the spirit in which we did it.

I love "proper" liturgy. By that I mean a Protestant adaptation of the Western or Roman rite. However, it is increasingly clear there are other ways to approach the worship of God, the proclamation of the Word, and the administration of the sacraments.

I have shared in authentic worship experiences that looked nothing like what Dom Gregory Dix described as the authoritative "shape of the liturgy." I remember participating in a eucharist that contained none of the classical rubrics for a proper service. Several members of our congregation had traveled from Chicago to Milwaukee to help a Father Groppi in his fight for racial justice in that northern community. Every Saturday he would gather as many people of good will as would come, and march them through the city with placards, leaflets, and singing. The effort had gone on for several months with few results—except the infuriation of those who lived in white ethnic neighborhoods. On the Saturday we arrived the atmosphere was steaming with hints of violence.

We gathered in the church, sang, and listened to the emotionally charged pep talks for which the civil rights movement was noted. The speeches were verbal dialogues between congregation and preacher. By noon the demonstration began. We marched through the friendly north side of town, and then we crossed to the south side—where segregation was the law, and residents were willing to defend their way of life to the death. Threats accompanied by bottles, rocks, sticks, and worse assaulted us along the route. Women and children were placed in the inner row of our three-abreast formations.

The march was scheduled to end at five o'clock at a parish hall where the sisters had prepared sandwiches and coffee. At five we marched by the church and kept on going! Six, seven, eight, nine, and still we marched, now by moonlight. At ten we made our way back to the parish hall, and found it dark. The hostesses had given up and gone to bed. A more wearied three hundred souls would have been hard to find.

Someone was roused. We entered the hall and sat silently on the floor, not from reverence but from exhaustion. The sandwiches, by now soggy, were located and distributed, along with cups of cold coffee. And someone said, "Let us give thanks to God." There followed a prayer whose content has been lost, but which I do remember was the centerpiece of an ecumenical eucharistic celebration. Christ was in our midst. We were in "koinonia," not only with those present but with angels and archangels and all the company of saints in heaven and on earth.

That day the Word was rightly proclaimed and the sacrament properly celebrated. Nobody asked whether a correctly ordained minister had presided, or if the prayer of consecration contained an invocation of the Holy Spirit, or even if what was consecrated was bread and wine. We, a community of faith called out from the world and dispersed back into the world within twelve hours, had broken bread, and in that act had found present in our midst the one who said, "This do in remembrance of me."

While we do not worship in order to conjure an emotional response—that would be manipulation—there was a moving of the Spirit with our spirits. Since we had asked the right question and performed the minor liturgy, the work of the people when they pray—the major liturgy being our ministry in the world— God had given us the extra gift.

Was the nature of this celebration, and those like it that we could all recite, only valid because it had occurred outside the strict boundaries of a parish? If what we do in worship, in a variety of forms, glorifies God, then the gift we receive may be that the world sees and believes. And if it does not, we have nevertheless praised God, and that is its own reward. Such is the nature of faithful worship in or out of a parish setting.

I may be terribly conservative. I feel deeply, sometimes to tears, when the great hymns of the church are sung, when the cross leads the banners in the procession, when with the proper words the bread is broken at the holy table, when the great pipe organ sings out the majesty of God. But there are many others who find our words and ceremonies boring. They are not touched, aesthetically, rationally, or emotionally.

If the church is doing authentic ministry in the world, God will give it the words for its prayers. And we may find those words shaped in ways we had not expected.

If we are to discover additional liturgical resources, where shall we look? We have discounted following those who ask the wrong question, "How can we be successful?" Nevertheless, just because "they" do it does not make it invalid. That would be as irrational as the political notion that if Communists find something to be true we must reject it on that basis alone.

Even while holding grave suspicions about how the new fundamentalists have trivialized worship, we may find in what they do authentic clues. If God listens to Bach and the angels to Mozart, the baroque-classical musical axis may not exhaust the way God can be praised. There is, for instance, much good contemporary music. Here I do not refer to the atonal sounds only a cultivated ear can enjoy, nor to the torch songs of the Jesus cult. The first do not elicit adoration from majorities in most congregations, and the latter are heretical.

Certainly we must improve the taste of church people. I remember returning to seminary after a weekend at my student church, complaining to my theological mentor that my people told me I was preaching over their heads. "Your task, young man, is to teach them to raise their heads!" he bellowed.

While that may be good advice, I doubt if of first importance is the increase of the congregation's love of the nine-tone scale. Nor is the task of parish leadership to insist on hymns that do not touch people at any positive place in their lives. Music, after all, is an aesthetic modality. While it teaches faith, music, particularly hymns, is a testimony to faith. Music addresses our non-rational sense of adoration and praise. While we do not want to perpetuate bad theology, there are gospel hymns and choruses that praise God aright. They are in the public domain and immediately available to us. Much new music also elicits the best of our religious feelings, and ought to be employed. Liberals, who are locked into their sturdy, gray, emotionally arid, liturgical cells, may succeed in asphyxiating congregations with layer after layer of flannel rationality.

Mainline churches might also look to other faithful Christians, whose liturgies have been life changing. For those of us who are white, I speak specifically of the black church, whose courage and faith during slavery, abolition, the civil rights movement, and today are an inspiration. While we must be careful not to stereotype, one finds a love of praise and sense of the holy in most black congregations. The assembly is not there to observe someone up front doing something. They are the worshipers. They respond to what is said with their bodies and voices.

Tales of the wild West had it that when cowboys came to church they were required to check their guns at the door. In many of our mainline white congregations one wonders if we have checked our bodies in the coat room before we enter. Not so in many black churches. During those times when I have preached in predominately black congregations, I knew there were folk out there—folk with voices, hands, feet, and deeply held commitments. I have rarely seen anybody nod off. There is hand clapping, not to congratulate a performer, but to exhibit what is being felt. God is worshiped with the body as well as the mind.

The point is this: In worship we must be willing to do a variety of very different things at their extremes. Along with our orderly services, where everything is spelled out, there must be room for the fresh moving of the Spirit, the unexpected and the unplanned. With our worship bulletins, orders of service, prayer books, and other printed materials, is there any room left for the unplanned, the spontaneous, and the unexpected? If it isn't in the bulletin God can't do it! Or at least a God who is a proper gentleman wouldn't dare.

There are other traditions rich in liturgical materials ready for our use. Perhaps the church has been most vital when it has been under persecution, or is in the midst of a self-cleansing. The letters, papers, and poems of Dietrich Bonhoeffer offer heartfelt cries to God.

While we tend to think of liberation theologians as fixated on frantic activity, there is a profound spirituality that undergirds and enriches the new forms of church life and commitment currently being generated in the Third World. A good example is the a compendium of spirituality by Gustavo Guiterrez, *We Drink from Our Own Wells* (Orbis, 1984).

Dullness sets in when the church puts on, almost totally, the protective coloration of its culture. Worshipers in many of our mainline congregations come knowing nothing startling is going to happen, and they leave convinced they were correct. Someone who wasn't present might still ask, "What did he say?," but few will ask, "What happened?" Where is the joy that breaks forth into singing? Where are the evidences that God has visited and redeemed the people? When do we know in our hearts, as well as in our minds, that bread has become a broken body and wine shed blood? When is there any profound communion between soul and soul? When is anyone's life profoundly changed? When does anyone hear, "In the name of Jesus of Nazareth, rise and walk"?

The third concern about worship in mainline congregations relates to the increased encroachment of the secular world on our turf. While we may have "In God We Trust" on our coins and insist we are a Christian nation, our official religion is secularism. Often the word "communism" is proceeded by the word "godless," but we live in the midst of godless capitalism.

The Constitution of the United States mandates a secular state. "Congress shall make no law regarding an establishment of religion" begins the first amendment. Nevertheless, during most of US history we have been dominated by a civil religion loosely connected with Christianity.

Consider how Sundays were treated. Until recent years, blue laws kept most businesses closed. Nor did much else go on until it was clear that worshipers had safely heard benedictions pronounced. We had little organized competition. While the golf courses and fishing holes were open, formal events were not held.

With the death of the blue laws, Sunday morning became an open season for whoever wanted the time. Sunday is now one of the biggest shopping days of the week. The crowd of cars around K-Mart far outstrips the vehicles lining the streets around the largest parish in town.

Among other Sunday morning events in my conservative community have been softball tournaments, ice hockey leagues, basketball games, lodge meetings, parades, bowling, automobile races, committee meetings, golf tournaments, dance recitals, family reunions, political rallies, and real estate closings. Add the advent of the ubiquitous weekend cottage and the extent of the problem becomes obvious. Half of the congregation is available for worship, and the other half is at work or play. Automatic loyalty is a thing of the past.

In an attempt to remedy this problem, we have attempted a number of alternatives. Catholics, who face the same competition, do well at Saturday afternoon masses. Efforts by Protestants to conduct services at alternate hours have been less than spectacular. People who have other things to do on Sunday mornings are not likely to show up on Thursday evenings.

Part of our problem is that most mainline churches flee from authoritarianism as if to utter "Thou shalt" would usher in the kingdom of Satan. As one thoughtful, conservative member of my congregation recently put it, "How is it we never hear about obedience anymore? Aren't there some things God still requires, like showing up for worship?"

The tradition of most mainline churches is steeped in freedom. No one speaks with authority. We have rejected the infallibility of both Holy Church and Holy Writ. Partly as a result of our Reformation heritage and partly flowing from the American ethos, individual choice has obtained doctrinal status. This passion for liberty and individualism has allowed us to be a vigorous, thoughtful people. But it has simultaneously ruled out even the most modest disciplines. Nobody has a right to tell anybody what they should or should not do. We are a voluntary society in which each volunteer sets his or her own terms. The resulting atomization has made the formation of disciplined communities difficult.

Most congregations have on their rolls scores, sometimes hundreds, of members who have no relationship to the church apart from their names appearing in a book. They never show up for worship, do not support the church financially, do not serve in her mission, do not hold to her faith. No one knows where they will be when the roll is called up yonder, but when it is called next Sunday down at old First Church they will be somewhere else. While many denominations have orderly procedures for determining who is a member and who is not, few congregations have the courage to exercise the option of disenfranchisement. We may occasionally conduct a campaign to reactivate the inactive, but these attempts are often frustrating and halfhearted. We have found it easier to recruit new members than to reactivate lapsed ones.

George may be a reprobate, a bigot, and he has vowed never to have anything to do with the church until death requires the presence of the minister, but take his name off the membership list and listen to his great aunt Sally raise an angry wail! As a voluntary society, we are hesitant to develop rules of conduct, and therefore we have no way to hold our members accountable.

The average congregation rarely sees more than half of its communicants at any service. Indeed, most established congregations never see 20 percent of their official book membership.

While we do not want to compromise our deeply rooted freedom of conscience, we need to come to terms with the meaning of discipline, accountability, and authority. Didn't we all make fundamental decisions about our priorities when we were baptized? Hasn't the church a responsibility to remind us of the loyalties we took on when we declared Jesus Christ to be Lord of our lives?

At the least there should be expectations that we are not too timid to articulate. Children suffer when there are no boundaries or when the boundaries are not defined. Nor do most adults rise much higher than the expectations set for them. If we seem to say, "It doesn't matter what you do on Sunday mornings," we will not win the loyalty of those who want religion to help them shape their priorities and their values.

Thus another dialectic is put into place: freedom and discipline. Without the tension generated when freedom strains against discipline, we will continue to be soft, flatulent, and effete. We may nag, scold, and play dog in the manger when our people are not present. But without boundaries clearly stated before the fact, worship will be treated casually, and the problem will grow worse.

Clues for the shaping of a religious discipline might come from the church under persecution. If the book of Galatians calls for freedom, the book of Revelation calls for order. In our own era, fewer more rigid disciplines have emerged than in the confessing church during Hitler's reign of terror. It may be out of style to hold one another accountable as did the faithful body of Christians described in Bonhoeffer's classic handbook for a covenantal community, *Life Together*. Nevertheless, any religious body facing, head on, the demands of the powers and principalities must develop a discipline if it is to survive.

The fourth liturgical issue concerns how we maintain authentic worship and yet find the sense of awe, excitement, and feeling that will capture the imaginations and hearts of those in our communities searching for a vital faith. How do we replace the aridity, which many modern people find in what we do, with a passion for the worship and service of God? How do we shape our prayers and praise so that those in our midst will declare, "I was glad when they said to me, 'let us go to the house of the LORD'" (Psalm 122:1)?

While liberals are proud of their ability to discover the untrod path, probe the unexplored theory, entertain the new notion, in the conduct of public worship we tend to be rigid, unyielding, and dry. "We have always done it this way" is an unwritten motto, and woe to the pastor who disturbs the order of worship a congregation has been using for the last fifty years or the denomination for the past two hundred.

During the 60s and early 70s, liberal churches were inundated by "experimental liturgies." Some were solid and some were silly. The church I served at the University of Chicago did both. I remember roping a dozen people together in order to make some obscure point about the nature of unity. On another occasion someone was wheeled out in a large plastic sack, and at the proper moment broke out of it. I believe the purpose was to make a point about birth. Once the youth, who were in charge of the service, ended it with the benediction from Porky Pig—"D-d-d-dats all, folks."

But if there was silliness there was also authenticity. A jazz band was present for the great celebrations, and a smaller string group called "The Sanctuary Band" regularly blended their softer tones with the great Skinner pipe organ in the praise of God. During one service, filmed and broadcast on the CBS evening news, we fashioned a "cross for urban man." (We had not yet understood the implications of inclusive language.) Two large "I" beams were obtained from the nearby steel mill. With a fountain of sparks showering the chancel, a welder fused the beams, and six strong men hung it above the altar. All of this done at a Sunday morning worship service, not at a Thursday evening committee meeting. That church had never had a cross—being the ultimate liberal congregation—and I was determined to put one in place. The simple wooden cross I had crafted and hung for the Lenten season had been taken down and burned by the property chairman the week after Easter. The great steel one still hangs in that building.

Beyond what we had planned, there were occasions when something unplanned took place, often the result of a personal need. On one occasion a young man, who had just received his induction notice and had been a longtime protester against the Vietnam war, appeared in an alcove over the chancel holding an upside-down American flag—a distress signal. "Help me!" he cried out. On another occasion a woman, who had just lost her children in a terrible custody fight, sobbed out her heart-wrenching story and was surrounded in a great congregational group embrace.

While experimental liturgies are out of style, I believe there is still room for the arting of worship which goes far beyond "what we have always done." The object is to praise God and declare the good news of Jesus Christ, not to titillate the audience. But God can be praised and Christ honored with feeling as well as with ideas. The dialectic between the worship of God with our minds and the worship of God with our hearts will provide the tension in which authenticity and faithfulness may be found.

Worship cannot be a side issue in the faithful congregation. It is at the center of everything else we do. Worship without the tension between old and new, mind and heart, freedom and discipline, will contribute to the demise of the mainline church. But those congregations willing to walk these critical boundaries will discover new modalities for the celebration of faith.

10

Lessons from Liberation

There is no more powerful living out of the gospel today then one finds among the wretched of the earth where liberation theology has taken root. How might the mainline church be reshaped and reformed using the insights of the world's oppressed? It is a mistake to romanticize the poor. Sin is no respecter of wealth. Neither is it a respecter of poverty. The poor are just as immoral, fragile, subject to greed and lust, as are the rest of us. Yet God has seemingly harbored a preferential option for them. Jesus, who "had no place to lay his head," made his home among them. It was the poor who heard him gladly.

We North Americans, who are among the world's affluent, cannot be liberationists, in the strict sense of the word. Liberation theology is essentially faith seen through and only through the eyes of the poor and the marginalized. No matter how we twist it, most of us are not oppressed. We can support them, stand in solidarity with them, attempt to redefine our own political and social perspectives, but we cannot even understand ways in which the gospel is heard by those who are required to make bricks without straw. Nevertheless, we mainline Christians have lessons to learn both from liberation theology and from the oppressed for whom liberationism has brought the good news of Jesus Christ.

Among areas ripe for exploration are (1) new forms of congregational life, (2) the place of the Bible in shaping the life of the religious institution, (3) the inevitable conflict between faith and the powers and principalities, (4) the centrality of praxis, and (5) the recovery of passion and joy.

First, let us examine ways that new forms of congregational life, which have sprung up among the Third World's poor, can inform the life and work of churches in the First World. Small groups of Christians variously known as base or basic Christian communities, or the church of the poor, have taken root wherever marginalized populations have rediscovered the power of the biblical imperative. While the social matrix in which these congregations flourish is substantially different from that found in most North American communities, making their adaptation problematic, the experience and structure of these new forms of witness provide important clues.

Mainline denominations face few more difficult problems than how to rescue from oblivion diminishing congregations in small rural communities with marginal economies. The farm crisis is now chronic. Rural people feel less and less in charge of their own affairs, and more and more at the mercy of banks, government agencies, large landowners, and a political climate in which they have been victimized.

Most denominations are making massive efforts to sustain these struggling outposts. The problem with our rescue projects is that they tend to use old patterns and systems that take enormous energy to keep going. But the more yoked parishes, lay ministers, workshops on the small church, and funds to keep them afloat, the more troubled the rural church seems to become. When in doubt, the mainline religious establishment tends to spend more money and produce more materials defining ways in which we have always done things. But turning up the volume on the record player does not change the tune. Since rural churches tend to be riveted to traditional ways of working, and since these ways no longer address the major problems, the issue is either radical transformation or slow death. Their problems will not be resolved by a perpetual subsidization. Ultimately answers must come from within, and they must be self-generating and self-sustaining.

The experience of basic Christian communities may offer a way out. Consider how they use buildings. Instead of being situated in old, hard to heat, inefficient structures, these new congregations meet in homes. Many of our rural parishes have dwindled to the point where a living room in a modest residence could comfortably seat the assemblage. Fifteen people in a home have the opportunity to become a community. Fifteen people in a church that seats a hundred is a testimony to despair. When the nature of the meeting place is dramatically changed there is a greater opportunity for what goes on to change. It is difficult to do a new thing in an old place—something about new wine and old wineskins.

Nor do these newly framed congregations need resident ministers, or even weekenders. One minister can serve as many as a dozen house churches. The life and work of the community of faith is vested in its people, not its clergy. The clergy are itinerate teachers and equippers. If funds are not used up for pastors' salaries, resources for staff, utilities, and upkeep on buildings, dollars will be available to help the parish accomplish its mission.

In our affluent churches, problems are often solved by renting paid workers. Do we need a better youth program? Add an employee with skills in youth ministry. Is the paperwork beyond the office staff? Add another secretary. And what people cannot get done, machines can! Among the poor, the rubric reads "Do it!" not "Buy it!"

It is the mission that is at the heart of the base community's life. This mission proceeds from the following theological assumptions: (1) God always stands with the dispossessed and the victimized; (2) God is united with them in their struggle for survival; (3) God wills that they be set free from their spiritual, political, economic, and social bondage; (4) God has called them to act together so that the freedom promised in Christ can be theirs; (5) their project is both spiritual and temporal, "religious" and political.

Instead of dealing only with the soul or with traditional religious symbols and ceremonies, as if these could be isolated from the rest of life, liberation becomes inclusive of every issue that inhibits humanness. "Integral liberation" does not distinguish quite so easily as we do between the sacred and the secular. It rather sees the divine mandate in broader terms. Powerlessness and faithlessness are equally outside the will of God.

Whenever the church meets, be it for Bible study, liturgy, the sacrament, or to address the common problems of farm foreclosures, government regulations, the loss of businesses in the communities, the gargantuan appetites of corporate interests, or the other oppressive problems facing rural people, it knows it is dealing with "religious" issues. The church touches every aspect of the community of faith. It is no longer a peripheral social institution with less and less impact on anyone's life or the life of the community. In my judgment, if the rural congregation grasps the lessons it can learn from base communities, it will become again a powerful force in the thousands of marginalized small towns in North America.

While the transmutation of traditional congregations into base Christian communities is a necessary step, I believe our existing marginal and marginalized congregations must also maintain a continuity with many of their traditional forms and ceremonies. Most base communities in Latin America are still self-consciously Catholic. A significant number of newly fashioned parishes in North America will be self-consciously Protestant, pietistic, and evangelical. When they meet they will sing many of the same hymns, read from the same Bible—although with a different understanding of Bible study, as we shall subsequently see—and perform the same rituals. They will understand that they are the church, not a political organization. At times the older, conservative ways of doing things will be in conflict with the radical new agenda and style. As long as they attempt to maintain liturgical continuity, while facing the world in newly minted radical ways, they will have the opportunity to flourish.

Not only can struggling congregations in farmland communities appropriate the insights of basic Christian communities, so can urban congregations experiencing a steady decline in strength. As the demographics of urban centers change, thousands of formerly aggressive mainline congregations have not known how to respond. Middle-class urban neighborhoods continue to experience the in-migration of racial and ethnic minorities, which tend to be far less affluent. We seem ill-prepared to receive them as our brothers and sisters. But then, they have not swarmed into our churches. They are often as uncomfortable with "us" as we are with them. Our worship styles, tight-knit fellowship circles, and friendship and kinship networks have not been appealing. The rule has been that congregations either relocate while they still have the strength to do so, or wither on the spot. If the building is still usable, it is eventually sold to a religious group that does have some sense of how to minister to these people. Insights from basic Christian communities may provide a fresh alternative.

Adapting the insights of these new ecclesial bodies to our experience need not be limited to parishes on the verge of oblivion. Strong congregations may find even more vigorous implications for their mission by spinning off a few small groups ready to explore new territory. Beyond what normally happens in small groups in the church, these set-aside units can develop their own liturgical and programmatic lives, while self-consciously remaining within the larger parish. If the congregation is not ready for radical alternatives, direct action, sharing resources, and taking risks, these smaller groups can be commissioned to test the borders of faith.

It is important that the dialectic be maintained by keeping them structurally integrated with the traditional congregation, so that the parish as a whole can profit from their experience. Sooner or later they may go their own ways. Many parishes may not be able to handle the implications of faith they will test. But after all, the congregation as we know it is not eternal, nor has it been ordained by God as the only way to organize witness and faith. We may discover a form of church life that will better serve us in the future. On the other hand, the witness of these small communities may help the larger congregation redefine its life and work.

The second lesson from liberation concerns Bible study. The failure of a vital biblical mandate may be at the root of much of the distress currently being experienced in the mainline church.

Almost every congregation I know has at least one, often several, class(es) of faithful people who have met together for fifty years, jumping up and down on ten verses a week, and coming out of that half-century of organized effort biblically illiterate. The chance that most of these groups will be able to do other than what they have always done is remote. They are essentially groups of old friends for whom the Bible study is their weekly "program." No effort should be made to disband these groups, or even to alter them. They meet vital social needs and are the most important "beyond-the-family" units that many people have.

In a number of more sophisticated congregations, Bible study may be taken in earnest as an academic or scientific discipline. A few thoughtful members may understand the synoptic problem, or the difference between lower and higher criticism. But all this knowledge seems to have little affect on their lives or their societies.

Or we may read two, three, or four lectionary selections at our regular services, but the words tend to pass right on by the assemblage without seriously affecting anyone.

Nowhere has Bible study been more neutralized than with our children. There is more to Christian education than learning to share toys. It is no wonder we have failed to rear a generation of radical Christians when we have protected them from the radical nature of the biblical record.

Liberation theology may help us find the life-changing nature of the biblical account once again. For liberation-oriented churches of the Third World, the Bible is the record of God's revolutionary activity. I have dealt at length with this issue in *A Guide to Liberation Theology for Middle-Class Congregations* (CBP Press). Suffice it to say here, when we understand that God is always at work among us, freeing the oppressed, releasing the captives, enlightening the blind, and proclaiming good news to the poor; that the Exodus is a permanent item on God's agenda; that the new birth in Christ is a remaking, not a readjusting; and that the church God has called out is a beachhead of the Kingdom, then we are in revolutionary territory. It is the Bible that sets that agenda. When it is seen as our marching orders, a call to action, not a deposit of doctrine, it is life changing.

For liberationists, the Bible is not a series of verses to be learned, information to be absorbed, points of view to be accepted, or historic occurrences to be believed, but a call to action. Orthopraxis replaces orthodoxy as the root of faith.

"Once we were Pharaoh's slaves in Egypt, and the Lord brought us out with a mighty hand!" That affirmation is our present condition as well as our heritage. Properly appropriated it comes to us in the present tense and in the imperative mood. Those who heard the message on the day of Pentecost responded not with "Isn't that interesting?" but with "What shall we do?" To be about the doing is at the center of authentic, biblically based church life.

The challenge is not to study the Bible so that we can be experts about its history and contents. Rather, liberating Bible study begins with a call to action. We assume before the fact that God has commissioned us to be a liberated and liberating community.

Any review of the literature produced by liberation theologians—particularly Latin Americans such as Gutierrez, Boff, Miranda, Echegaray, Bonino, and others—will show quickly and clearly the way this action-oriented approach to Bible study reforms and renews Christians who take it seriously. I am not optimistic that congregations wholesale will find the methodology appealing. My hope is that there are enough people of faith and courage in almost any congregation willing to take the leap and become the leaven in the ecclesiastical lump. Such leaven, it must be noted, will prove more explosive than insidious.

Congregations that take the biblical imperative to heart should be prepared for tension. Ministers who see their primary task as keeping the peace, or consider internal harmony to be the most cherished ecclesial reality, are well advised to stay away from the kind of Bible study that goes on in liberated communities of faith. When the time comes to march, all the troops may not be ready. Indeed some may decline the invitation or quit the service. While we wait patiently for the slower to get up to speed, when the day of march arrives we move out, realizing not everyone will be with us.

The third lesson of liberation theology concerns the inevitable conflict between the Kingdom for which we hope and the principalities and powers with which we live. Or to put it in action terms, the church continually seeks to define human freedom in a way that will trouble those in power. One assumes that those who control wealth and the decision-making apparatus which generates it will resist efforts to alter the balance in such a way that not only goods and services but even power is more equitably distributed.

In the teachings and parables found in the synoptics, Jesus made the same point over and over again. The reign of God does not look like the kingdoms of this world. There is, in fact, a radical discontinuity between Kingdom ethics and worldly ethics. In the reign of God, the last come first and the first last; the irresponsible son gets the ring, the robe, and the party; the Samaritan is the hero; those who work one hour are paid as much as those who work all day; the meek inherit the earth; peacemakers are blessed; God continually sides with the outcasts, the weak, and the non-persons.

I once had the honor of sharing several hours with Gustavo Gutierrez. One of our small group asked him to define non-persons, a term he repeatedly used. He recalled that the day Oscar Romero was martyred, seven other activists were gunned down by Salvadorian death squads. "Everybody knows the name of Oscar Romero, but nobody knows the names of these other seven. They have no names. They were only counted. There were seven, and that is all we know about them. To be a number and not a name is to be a non-person, and the world is full of non-persons."

The Kingdom is inhabited by non-persons to whom God has given a new name, who indeed have become God's special sons and daughters. When God sides with these non-persons, the poor and marginalized, God becomes the enemy of those who want no alteration in how power is distributed. The powerful are most often only comfortable in a world where there are masses of non-persons. Their greatest threat is that they will be required to share the wealth and the power that has previously set them apart.

Liberation theology holds that the fundamental mission of the church is not to save souls but to be the voice of the voiceless. Beyond the testimony of the words it proclaims, a liberating and liberated church is the arm of God equipped to act out good news to the poor, release to the captives, sight to the sightless, and liberty to the oppressed. That is what Jesus announced as his mission, and it is the mission of those whom God has called out and commissioned in every age.

When God's people take up the cause of the wretched of the earth, they are bound to be in conflict with the powerful. When the rulers of this present age are also members of our churches, the site of the conflict moves from the world to the religious institution itself. The problem that most often pertains, however, is not that liberation theology divides parishes, but that we are so willing to water down the Christian imperative in order to preserve the peace and harmony of the congregation that we neither hear nor do we even proclaim the gospel.

In creative congregations there will be conflict, tension, the clash of opposing ways of thinking and doing. Instead of retreating from the tension, it should be celebrated. For herein lies the raw material for the generative dialectic. It is in the tension that the new, the creative, and the life changing are hammered out. Those parishes willing to accept and deal with the dialectic will discover afresh the power of faithful word and commissioned deed. Those who settle for what is safe and harmless will never even hear the echoes of the thunder that rolls across the skies when the Kingdom is on the way.

A fresh look at theological education is called for. Clergy who are taught that it is their role to be peacemakers will find it difficult to understand that the sword Christ came to bring has been put in their hands. Jesus held that it was not for use against enemies on the outside, but that the division will be within the family itself. Newly trained clergy will know how to allow conflict to develop because they will understand the biblical imperative in proclaiming the Kingdom. No better training is available than that which is to be found as we sit at the feet of the poor of the Third World, and the theologians who articulate the gospel for them and for the rest of the church as well.

The fourth lesson of liberation is the recovery of Christian praxis as the foundation stone of parish life. While not a common word in our vocabularies, the term "praxis" is widely used by liberation theologians. It denotes faithful action of a particular kind. It is action that is life- and society-altering. It sees faithfulness not in terms of proper belief but in terms of liberating activity. It is political as well as spiritual. It begins with the premise that God has set the oppressed free, and it endeavors to act out that presupposition. Liberating praxis celebrates the coming reign of God and gives evidence that it is at hand.

When liberationists are often accused of believing in works righteousness, they respond that the very notion comes from a time when the debate centered on scholastic theological issues, but that such an era is gone. Today there is only one call on faithful people. And that is a call to liberating action. Let others debate doctrinal obscurities. When the oppressed are set free there will be time to do speculative theology. For now, it is orthopraxis, not orthodoxy, that lies at the root of faithfulness.

While many of us steeped in academic theology will have a difficult time with that way of seeing and experiencing the gospel, the call to liberating activity with and on behalf of the oppressed will come as a breath of fresh air in congregations smothered by ideological concerns. If liberation theology is taken seriously, the church will again become a place where something happens. And what happens will change lives!

We are not suggesting that all reflection be eliminated, and that all theologizing must be done en route, only that the *best* theologizing will be done en route—and that all theologizing must be done in the tension that exists between reflection and action.

In a religious environment dominated by classes, workshops, study groups, committees, boards, seminars, study guides, conferences, conventions, lectures, and think tanks, a solid infusion of hands-on doing the gospel is bound to be redemptive. Groups of young people can spend Sunday evenings from now until they are gray headed studying the mission of the church. But send them to a work camp for a week among the marginalized and they will come back changed.

Talking about feeding the hungry is a middle-class luxury. The act of feeding the hungry is redemptive. Even more redemptive is the act of reordering society so that power as well as wealth is redistributed, and the hungry have an opportunity to feed themselves. Charity is, after all, only a way station on the road to justice. While we tend to be more comfortable with doing charitable acts—which leave us in ultimate control—than we are with reordering systems, justice only comes about through the latter. Even so, even charity is better than studying about the number of children who will starve in Ethiopia—or is this year's focus on the Sudan? As the hungry are being fed the meaning of what is being done will be clarified.

If just a small portion of the time spent sitting and listening could be redirected toward action on behalf of and with the oppressed and the marginalized, there would be a revival of faith within our congregations. When has the church been the strongest? When it has been about the mission of Christ. I am not advocating thoughtlessness. I am suggesting, however, that the most appropriate and powerful reflection takes place in the context of doing the truth.

"How do you know what to do? Isn't it better to figure out where you are headed before you start out?" Such are the queries directed at those who insist that action precedes rational discourse. Obviously I believe in rational discourse. Otherwise, why write books?

For many years I wanted to learn to sail. I read every "how-to" book in the library. I subscribed to magazines on the subject. I knew the history of sailing, the physics of how the wind moves the boat, the rules of navigation. But few of these things held any power until I got on a sloop and made my way to the open sea. THEN I went back and read the same books I had previously digested, and at last understood and internalized what had been only academic and peripheral.

It is impossible for members of our churches to grasp the liberating power of the gospel as long as they are content to study the subject. Nor does theological sophistication make one a Christian. Only doing the truth is salvific. No one can be an authority on love who has not loved, or been loved. While the church must continue to be a community that thinks and thus believes, if it hears the imperative of liberation theology what it thinks will be discovered in the context of what it does.

Liberation's fifth lesson concerns the recovery of passion and joy in the Christian experience. The terms "praxis," "project," and "marginalized" have a pedantic sound. It all seems like such a grim business. Indeed the struggle for freedom is a grim business. But at the same time it is a joyful and passionate experience. What can be more joyful than to be set free? Because Christianity is essentially a liberating faith, it has traditionally been an aesthetically powerful faith. Music, as well as the rest of the arts, flourish in the faithful community. The Hebrew people came out of Egypt singing, and we have been singing ever since.

I have never been in the midst of people committed to liberation who were not a lively, energetic, passionate, and joyful community. In the most wretched circumstances, where one would least expect to experience mirth, there is laughter and passion. Dominique Laperrier, a French journalist, has written about the most desperate and oppressed community in the slums of Calcutta. He calls it *The City of Joy* (Doubleday, 1985).

Can we say our congregations are as joyful? Is our singing robust? Would someone coming into our churches be taken by the obvious sense of expectancy in the lives of those seated in the pews? Occasionally I have looked from the chancel on a congregation in the midst of its "celebration" of the mighty acts of God, and have been puzzled by the lack of any visible sign of positive emotion. Even singing looks to be a painful experience. Half of the congregants have not even taken the trouble to open a hymnal. Many of those who have are singing as if they were in some modest discomfort. A few are smiling, but not many. One wonders what has become of the sense of passion in the gospel? Let them sit at the feet of the oppressed. Let them learn to be joyful in the Lord. Let our congregations become once more places of passion.

While passion can cycle down into fanaticism, the failure of feeling can sink slowly into despair and death. I doubt if the typical mainline parish can be accused of fanaticism. We are middle-class middle-Americans, stuck in the middle of the road. The last thing we want to be accused of is being radical. We have so totally adopted the protective coloration of society that to be out of step with whatever happens to be the cultural norm is our greatest fear. We are careful not to do anything with much gusto.

Whatever can be said of the gospel, it is not dull! To the extent we have made it dull, denatured it, taken the joy from it, we are in apostasy. As we encounter our liberated and liberating brothers and sisters in the Third World, or even the oppressed in our midst, their best gift to us may be the recovery of joy and passion which are hallmarks of authentic faith.

11

New Issues for a New Age

There is often a fine line between being current and being trendy. The church must continually evaluate whether the issues with which it deals are substantial matters affecting human existence, or simply the latest fad. Congregations have often spent enormous amounts of money designing buildings that incorporate the most recent architectural styles, only to discover that in a decade what they did was not contemporary, just dated and boring.

A dozen years ago there was great enthusiasm in our community for a particular brand of percussion instruments to be used in work with children. Someone was employed by the public schools to teach music educators the wonders of Orff technology. Our congregation raised almost $2,000 to buy the entire line. After a few "performances" the fad passed and we now have a closet full of these very expensive but seldom used gadgets.

Issues that seem hot today may be cold tomorrow, as may be theological styles. I have lived through a score of them, all the way from a fascination with Eastern mysticism to the death of God. Nevertheless, the risk of being quickly out-of-date should not keep us from responding to emerging concerns.

What are the issues to be addressed as we move toward the turn of the century, and how does an aggressive church respond to them? Consider the ecological issue with all its ramifications, the breaking out of new peace initiatives, the newfound dignity of women, the failure of the Marxist experiment, the growing concern with AIDS, the increased secularization of American life, new dimensions of a global economy, a collection of New Age concerns, cultural pluralism, the intermingling of world religions. What is the relationship between these and similar issues and the work of the parish? What are the theological imperatives and how do we address such vital matters while staying faithful to our fundamental mission?

The thesis of this book is that we do so head-on and without equivocation. The reluctance of mainline churches to deal aggressively with the important agendas before the world's people will commit us increasingly to the sidelines. While an entire book can, and should be, spent reflecting on these concerns, for purposes of illustration we will deal only with two that encompass many of the most vital matters: the New Age movement and the environment.

Consider first what has been called the New Age movement. To some it is the world's best hope. To others it is a satanic plot. Fundamentalists see it as the Antichrist. A prominent TV personality, speaking to fifteen hundred members of the religious right said, lowering his voice to a whispery warning, "It's modified Hinduism....It's sweeping into American business, and American classrooms....It's blatant demonism and young people are its target." Well, if it's blatant demonism we ought to know about it, this New Age movement. Despite these attacks, the New Age movement focuses a number of concerns important to a young generation, concerns the mainline church will avoid at its own peril.

The New Age movement was born in reaction to America's fascination with technology—our real religion. "Science is our shepherd, we shall not want." But with the worship of science came a drying up of spiritual values. No need to pray for God's help, just turn technicians loose. This American mind set, ubiquitous in the 60s, was complicated by a terrible war—the first

American defeat. Vietnam had sapped the American will and left a generation bitter and disillusioned. It was an arid time for things spiritual.

Young people, hungering for meaning, looked to the church but found little nourishment there. Churches were too concerned with preserving their traditions, bowing to the needs of well-to-do older people, and protecting their turf. So these young people turned to whatever sources of spiritual nourishment they could find. They might have turned to alcohol, but their parents had leaned on that drug, and they were not about to cotton to anything their parents loved. But other materials produced altered states of consciousness, and the guru of the movement, Timothy Leary, had told them they could find inner peace with chemicals—and they believed him.

More traditional young people sought meaning in transcendental meditation and forms of pop psychology. A decade before, one might have found young people crowding auditoriums to demonstrate for peace. Now these groups could be put in a telephone booth, and the large meeting rooms were filled with young people going "OOOOOOHHHMMMMMMMMM."

Aging hippies, left over from the psychedelic days, were sitting naked in tubs of hot water in Esalen, California, trying to get themselves together. Many of them are still being par boiled but are no more together than they were when they started. Still others sought help in Indian Gurus. A few of the more fragile turned to the Moonies or gave themselves to other esoteric cults. The tame settled for encounter groups.

The sum total of these efforts—and a few even more bizarre things we will mention below—became known as the New Age movement. At root it was a reaction to the religion of scientism, the emotional breakdown America went through in the wake of the Vietnam war, and the failure of traditional churches to meet the inner needs of a young generation.

Whenever there are that many people searching for something new, with a few dollars to spend trying to find it, there will arise those who know what to do. Experts, gurus, shamans, spirit guides, and group leaders arrived by the score ready to trade their wisdom for whatever the market would bear. Scientology and EST are just two such groups. People pay big bucks to spend a weekend sitting on the floor getting belittled and shouted out. It is supposed to tap some inner resource. It taps their back pockets.

The more mundane turned to astrology. A recent survey indicates that nearly a fourth of the American people and almost half of all Californians regularly consult astrologers. Even the wife of the President was determined to arrange her husband's schedule on the basis of the planets.

Then came Shirley McLaine with tales of reincarnation, inhabiting other physical bodies, and channeling—in which a medium goes into a trance and becomes the voice of someone long dead. Others, less exotic, clutch crystals or sit under pyramids, all the time insisting that anybody who believes "God so loved the world he gave an only son" is superstitious and gullible. While 42 percent of Americans told surveyors they have recently talked to someone who is dead, many of these same people have turned away from the Christian faith because they could not believe Jesus ever even lived.

There are still big bucks to be made in the New Age movement. Traditional religion may not be in favor among the sophisticated and the knowing, but superstition is alive and well. I doubt that the New Age movement is the new creation Jesus talked about in our gospel lesson, or the new heaven and new earth pictured in the book of Revelation.

Is the New Age movement therefore the foe of faith? While it is not the satanic image some say it is, I believe authentic faith is always wary of superstition, whether it is evidenced outside the church or in it.

But there is another side to the New Age movement that I believe to be an ally, not an enemy, of our faith. Remember that the movement arose out of a spiritual hunger—a need churches were not filling. Many of the answers to life are not to be found in test tubes or telescopes, in laboratories or think tanks, because the important problems are spiritual. The basic issues are to be addressed in the inner search.

If the church has lost touch with the power of meditation, the mystery of the soul, and the value in imaging the good and the beautiful, the New Age movement has not only reminded us of our spiritual bankruptcy, but has also met needs we have left unmet. We are a frantic people, and if meaning can be found in inner disciplines long known in Hindu and Buddhist religions, God may allow us to learn life's important lessons there. If the war cry of modern Westerners is "Don't just stand there, do something," perhaps we need to hear the gentler advice of Eastern religions, "Don't just do something, stand there—or kneel there." It may be the New Age reminds us again of the power of prayer. God often uses those of other folds to teach us when, in our formalism, we have forgotten how to hear God's voice.

If we are now in the presence of a generation hungry for the re-emergence of spiritual values, disciplines, and perspectives, how does the typical congregation address these insights and concerns? First, we take them and those who raise the issues seriously. People hungry for spiritual depth, who want to fill the great plastic void created by a technological society, may form the core of a whole new way to be the church. Having turned them and their hunger away, the mainline church has seen them quickly slide into fundamentalism, with its esoteric languages, evocative styles, and emotional power. Welcoming them, and exploring with them the ways of the spirit, may be one of the great hopes of a dusty, dry, all-too-cerebral religious desert in which much of the mainline church is dying of thirst.

We may have passed through the time when ministers saw themselves as executive directors of small not-for-profit businesses, or psychologists, or program directors, or social engineers. We may begin to realize we have always been in the spirit-guide business. The main issues most folk confront are questions of depth, and the main hungers deal with the inner life. Allies from the New Age movement may help us re-orient ourselves so we can reclaim our purpose and rechart our course.

A second cluster of issues gathers around ecological and environmental concerns. Seen at one level, this is a scientific matter, but seen at a deeper level, it is a theological matter. There may be no more important concern in the decades to come than how we treat our mother, the earth. We need to be reminded that the earth is one large ecosystem, and we humans are only a tiny part of it. We were not put here to exploit the rest of nature but to live in harmony with it. All of life is sacred, not just human life.

If denuding the virgin forests of Oregon eradicates the spotted owl, we need to think long and hard about destroying that forest, for the spotted owl is part of God's sacred creation. Either we care for our mother or we shall all be destroyed.

Everything is related to everything else in this ecosphere. If electric companies are trying to convince us that laws to protect the air from the junk we throw into it are too expensive, a carefully articulated and lived-out faith proclaims that if the air goes, we all go! The Bible promises a new and better earth for all God's creatures, and the church must be the basic proclaimer of that verity and vision.

We are not just physical bodies. We are souls and spirits. We not only eat and sleep, we dream and pray and imagine. If the scientific world addresses ecological concerns only from the perspective of the left brain—the mathematical, rigid, systematic, no-nonsense part of who we are—authentic faith can introduce to the conversation the right brain: the source of creativity, art, poetry, spirituality, religion, and grace.

If there is a concern about recycling, conservation, the preservation of the natural resources of a region, and the other rudimentary ground rules for the care of spaceship earth, the mainline church ought to be the center of those concerns. The time to become involved is at the beginning, not at the end, of the parade. Throughout Christian history the church has often been the first to speak and to act, but in our era a more careful, hesitant and almost hopelessly befuddled religious institution has often been the last to speak and act, if we speak and act at all.

Almost every movement for human good and the preservation of life has been financed, peopled, and ideologically supported by the mainline church. Count them up: the abolition movement, the organized labor movement, the child labor movement, the civil rights movement, the peace movement, the women's rights movement. Take from those struggles the money and the personnel the church has provided and you will have successfully gutted them. A failure of nerve tempting us to shy away from the agenda God has placed before the world is the quickest path to decay and death. Having been frightened by our loss of numbers and effectiveness, the temptation has been to do exactly the wrong thing. We have grown cautious, conservative, and timid. Our salvation may lie in the opposite direction. When we again become bold, "radical," clear, and action oriented, we will rediscover who we are and what God would have us be. The alternative is a continuation of the slow sad decline we have experienced for a generation.

There are satanic forces in the world—forces of hate and cruelty, forces that can destroy the natural world and mutilate the spiritual world. Insofar as the church wallows in superstition it will be under the judgment of God and of history. But insofar as we boldly reaffirm not only our right but our responsibility to set the agenda for a larger world we may rediscover our zest for life, our creativity, and our hope.

Called from our one-dimensional selves into the inner world of the spirit and the outer world of concerns for the earth, we may find our mission again and resonate with God's own voice.

12

Come Life or Death

It is human nature to fend off death. "Everybody wants to go to heaven, but nobody wants to die." With the amazing discoveries of medical science and gerontology have come the corollary of an unproductive lengthening of life. For many, certainly, the latter years have not only been made longer but better. But we have also learned how to preserve the biological functions long after all meaning has gone.

I recall a six-month fight by a woman to keep her husband alive when it had become clear he would never again regain consciousness. He could not even experience pain. Had it not been for tubes, wires, and assorted machines, which kept the heart and lungs going, he would have peacefully died. It was not that she held out hope he would recover or that the condition could be reversed. She only wanted to keep him with her as long as she could. The bill was a million dollars. But the financial costs were the small part of the price this final illness exacted from the family.

As the tension mounted so did the arguments. The physicians became increasingly unwilling to let the situation continue. When the hospital finally decided it would not sustain him any longer, and the body was allowed to cease its minimal functions, not a member of the family was speaking to any other member.

All of us could recite similar experiences. As strong as is the power of death, the thirst for a shred of life, no matter how fragile, is just as strong. But death is a normal, God-ordained part of life. Faith and courage welcome the enemy God has translated into a friend. Whether we live or die we are the Lord's.

And if our individual lust for life, even in extremes, is strong, equally as strong is our commitment to keep our institutions going. As there are breathing corpses, lying in intensive care units month after month, there are also institutions kept artificially alive when all meaning and purpose has long since been terminated. There is an institutional inertia that demands ventilators, wires, and tubes. If at one time the body could have been allowed to expire courageously, in command of its own demise and with some sense of celebration, we tend to hold on and on, and it finally "slips away" abandoned and lonely. I don't suppose I want to live the non-life of a mechanically sustained cadaver when all my relatives, loved ones, and friends are long gone and I die in isolated and uncared-for exile. And neither should a religious institution come to its final days in that deplorable circumstance.

Consider congregations so placed they are no longer able to sustain anything that could be called ministry. In a small town in the Midwest there are eight congregations, all kept going by machines—endowments, denominational support—all living in an ecclesiastical intensive care unit. By the time this book is in print at least two of them will probably have expired, their buildings abandoned, their windows objects of vandals, and what was left of their congregations bewildered and bitter. There will be no formal celebration of their ministries, nothing preserved for history, no words said over them, no declaration they had touched the lives of people with the grace of God. One Sunday morning nobody will show up to unlock the doors and their existences will have unceremoniously come to an end.

Long before that dismal day, a congregation might have taken every penny in its account and had a marvelous going-out party to which every person who had ever been remotely connected with the parish had been invited. Whatever remained could have been turned over to the judicatory, liquidated, and used for the service of humankind and the further glory of God. Or years prior to death, three or four of these congregations might have realized the town itself was fading away and the maintenance of eight congregations was not only unnecessary but bad stewardship: eight furnaces blasting away on Sunday mornings, eight light bills, eight part-time ministers to sustain. Someone might have had the vision to determine that the strength of these tiny units could be multiplied if they combined resources. The result might have been two or three effective parishes. While this has happened in a number of communities, the rule seems to be that people would rather lose their church buildings to decay and rot than lose them in a merger. "We'll join up just as long as we do it in our building!"

The scenario depicted above is not limited to rural congregations and communities. Just as many still-breathing parishes, long since having lost their lust for life, are kept going in cities by a few good souls who just can't see them closed. While none of us have the right to say what anyone should do about the death of a loved one, common sense demands some better remedy than long-term intensive care. Not that an institution ought to call it quits when it can find new ways to health, vigorous ministry, and renewed purpose. In most cases the answer lies in discovering the dialectic through which resuscitation can take place and many additional years of productivity can be had. It is hoped that this book might be one resource for congregations wondering if their disease is terminal.

While it is true that thousands of tiny congregations—and some not so small—will cease to exist by the turn of the century, I am not predicting the death of the parish as a primary manifestation of religious life. I do not believe that the house-church movement or other new forms of the worshiping community will replace the traditional congregation. But even if that should happen it would not the mean the end of faith. After all, the parish is not derivative of a mandate written eternally in heaven. Christian parishes have their roots in the synagogue. But the synagogue only came into being because of a change in sociological and political circumstances. Dispersed Jews could no longer travel easily to the temple in Jerusalem, and the synagogue was a necessary modification in the way the tradition was handed down from generation to generation. As needs changed, so did the shape of the institution. The precious cargo was not to be confused with the vehicle that carried it. It is not our craft that is sacred, only what it bears from age to age and place to place.

If the dispersion produced the synagogue, and the synagogue is the historic parent of the parish, who knows what changes in the world will or are already calling for in terms of new ways to organize the faithful. My crystal ball is no better than anyone else's, but while I don't predict the demise of the parish, I stand ready to celebrate any new form of witness, mission, and worship God has for us. God is the same yesterday, today, and forever, but any religious institution which thinks it shares that divine attribute is already terminal.

Nor do I believe we will be taken over by fundamentalism—not unless we voluntarily succumb, having been lured to the rocks by the seductive call of success. The lust for mass appeal may drive a few into the jaws of irrationality. A reaction to secularism may bring on a new age of conservative religion, but what phases in, historically, will eventually phase out again.

Sailing one day near a seemingly harmless shore, I misjudged the depth of the water and felt the keel of the boat dig into a sandbar. All the traditional efforts to dislodge it proved futile: rocking the boat, backing the mainsail, setting an outboard anchor. Checking my chart to determine what might have accounted for my error in judgment, I discovered I had misread the tides. I thought the tide was high, which would have provided two or three feet of safe passage over the sandbar. But in that part of the bay the tide pulls back earlier than I had predicted.

The further the tide ebbed the more deeply embedded we became. Finally the boat heeled until the hull was resting on its side. I would have been in considerable distress had I not realized that what goes out soon comes in. In that part of the world, tides run ten feet. Every six hours the water floods in, and in the next six leaves again. All I could do was wait for a natural event over which I had no control. Sure enough, in due time the waters returned, the boat righted itself, and we were able to float out.

I am convinced the fundamentalist tide is not only a predictable cyclical occurrence, it is a fluke of history. No one can long turn back the clock of science, history, or thought. While keeping the institution—the parish—in as good a repair as possible, our task is to wait for the turning of the tide of history. We cannot force the tide, conjure it, or wish it away. What we can do is allow ourselves to be stretched by the various sets of polarities and tensions as they present themselves, and find the new synthesis for the brighter day that will surely dawn.

Or it may be that the breezes have already changed and we have not yet reset the sails. While God is consistent, the winds of history are not. Institutions that can only move in one direction under one set of winds die off. My deepest feeling is that mainline denominations and their parishes—anchored solidly in the traditional ways of working and worshiping, but holding those old ways in dialectical tension with the new and radical—will emerge even stronger when the waters move once again.

But whatever, life is not finally in our hands but in the hands of the master of the winds and tides, to whom be glory now and forever.